What Men Are Saying About
What It Takes

What It Takes moves deeply into men's too easily denied struggles and invites them to come out of hiding into Gospel freedom, as men! Of the many books on Christian manhood, this one—intensely practical and insistently biblical—is one of the best.

~ **Dr. Larry Crabb**, *author, psychologist, Director of New Way Ministries*

American men are in crisis. Truthfully, all of American society is in a state of crisis, but strong men are key to leading us out of it. Many do not know where to find the tools they need to develop the strong character traits and package of virtues required to do the job.

What it Takes is an excellent primer to help men get started. In a world where many fathers have been absent or weak, younger men need strong mentoring to become men of valor such as they may have never seen in their homes growing up. Others may have had good fathers, but still hide in the shadows because current American society, from the media to our government to our education system, often diminishes the idea of a strong man controlling his passions, leading his family or even having a family.

Men need self confidence. Even more, they need a clear light shining on the small steps that they must navigate daily in order to win the larger battles in life. In a culture filled with temptations that degrade character and derail destinies, they need a robust protection system to help them guard against the "termites" that can rot the insides of their character, even while they maintain a brave facade.

This book takes men on such a journey.

I highly endorse **What It Takes** and its author, whom I have known for many years. He knows what he is talking about. He has shed the tears and celebrated the victories that accompany true Christian manhood. Even more, he has led hundreds of men to the right path and equipped them for the battles of their lives.

This is a book for our times. Men, take it up and go forward.

~ **Alan Eason**, *Webmaster at The Stream and Principal at AE communications*

~ ~ ~

Have you ever asked, "what does it mean to be a man?" Then **What It Takes** is that book you have been looking for. In a world that strives to blur the definition of manhood, this book helps to recenter what it means to be a man through biblical teaching, personal stories, and unique observations by the author. This is an excellent book for individual reading or for groups of men that have decided they want to learn from others what it means to be a man of God. All men desire to know if they have what it takes. This book is an excellent tool to help men understand that, with a relationship with Jesus, they do have what it takes to succeed in all aspects of their lives.

~ **Judah Wilkins**, *UT-BATTELLE, Export Control Analyst*

~ ~ ~

I love stories of redemption because it is what God does best. The twelve men who shared their personal stories of redemption make this a powerful read. Lance invites us to take a journey with him in **What it Takes** and it is a journey men should courageously pursue.

~ **Daniel Harris**, *former CFO, Knoxville Wholesale Furniture*

~ ~ ~

In my experience of leading men's ministries, one truth stands out—Every man is struggling with spiritual issues, be it pornography, marital infidelity, pride, anger, doubts, materialism, and so forth. **What it Takes** uses powerful personal testimonies skillfully interwoven with scripture references and punctuated with thoughtful questions to help men think deeply about their spiritual condition and their relationship of love for Lance who writes as one who has been "in the trenches." His personal fight for the souls of men has resulted in this powerful and practical book. **What it Takes** will change the life of any man who dares to work through it with a heart that is open to the Father.

> ~ **Dr. David Duncan**, *Senior Vice-President and Program Director Oak Ridge Associated Universities*

What it Takes provides a relevant and relatable message for all men, while inspiring a call to meaningful manhood. As the enemy strikes men down, this read lifts them up with truths, as they fight to leave the past behind and seek a new life with Christ as the center. Life's battles are real, and we need authentic men to break passivity and lead more than ever before! This read equips men with the spiritual armor their hearts long for, to move them past strongholds and propel them toward living a life of purpose.

> ~ **Kris Cline**, *Regional Director Washington and Oregon, Cellular Sales*

What It Takes is not just another "how to" book based upon an institutional definition of manhood. Rather, it is a snapshot of real life experiences of men and contains the right questions, based upon Biblical truths, that if followed, will guide a man toward Authentic Manhood.

At the core level, this book brings to center stage the manhood of Christ and how authentic manhood can only be achieved by walking with Jesus every day.

We live in a world of "impressions, appearances, pretends and fakes." Authentic is often defined as "not false or copied, genuine or real". The real life stories shared in Lance's book describe men who were first moved by the Holy Spirit for self-evaluation, which led to repentance, before they began to understand what authentic manhood really is, as defined God.

What It Takes is written by an authentic man, Lance Cooper, who knows first hand and from experience what it means to "face the wound and the fear" and prevail through a daily walk with Christ.

If you don't read this book, better yet, embrace it, you will miss a great journey. Buy the book.

~ **Harlan Goan**, *Executive VP, FreedomLink RX LLC*

~ ~ ~

Having spent the last twenty years of my life with Lance Cooper as a friend and business partner, I have always admired his passion for changing the lives of men and inspiring others to greatness. He has walked a long journey with God through fields of joy and behind the woodshed of discipline. I am so thankful for his gift of writing and teaching, and his strong desire to help others avoid mistakes that keep men mired in the mud of mediocrity instead of living a life of joy and productivity. **What It Takes** is a mix of information about why men struggle, answers to the struggles and challenges of men, and an inspiring journal of stories that can move all men to healing and a more fruitful journey.

~ **Steve Suggs**, *Partner and Chief Operating Officer, SalesManage Solutions*

~ ~ ~

This book began as a series of messages I hoped would move men to connect with God. A couple of years ago, I felt a need to send an email message a day to a group of men for a forty day period to have them reflect on their lives and their behaviors as men. Please read what men said who received those emails.

What Men Said About the 40 Days of Emails that Began *What It Takes*

I think this one is speaking directly to me. I've got to learn to forgive myself for poor choices and know that they're not what makes me a man. I've been having a really tough time the past several weeks and your messages have been great. I think one thing I didn't understand (and will continue to learn) is the TRUE meaning of marriage. I didn't grow up in a spiritual household and respectfully, didn't have the best role models anywhere in my life. I want to make sure my family grows up in a better environment than I did. I have a lot to learn and I know that I can't do it alone. I would like to talk to you about this but honestly, I can't control my emotions enough (I have tears in my eyes just typing this) to be able to do it just yet but I'm working really hard at it. I've struggled with anxiety my entire life and finally, I'm going to address it and work towards learning how to manage it. I have a doctor's appointment this afternoon at 3 and I hope with a little help, I can get it under control. Keep the messages coming and thanks for everything!

Thanks for the devotional Lance. This one really hits home. I have had an exhausting several days. Lack of sleep. So many demands. Also, fear of the future has entered into the equation recently. I have been feeling a bit sorry for myself. This devotional is exactly what I needed. Thanks again.

— — —

Just want to let you know that your emails have given me and others strength and I have used them for people who have reached out to me in the past week and a half. In the time since we talked, I've had 4 people whom I'm very close with reach out to me over something going on in their lives. Some of the things that they've come to me with, I've been able to refer to the emails you've sent as they have related with the issue. Even bringing some men to tears that are not the "sensitive" type. With the words that God is placing on your heart to write, I have been able to use His words spoken through you for guidance and encouragement to those that have reached out to me. I really appreciate your devotion to writing these. May God bless you as you do these. He is using them for His benefit!

— — —

Today's message was great because we do act like what we think. Thoughts turn into beliefs. Then those turn into actions. You could have bad thoughts like Hitler and decimate a race and ruin much of Europe, or you could have godly thoughts like Martin Luther and re-introduce true Christianity to the world. Keep up the good work, God is using you to encourage a lot of men!

— — —

I have been reading with enthusiasm each of your daily posts. I have yet to reply because I am assuming that you are not asking for a reply, and that your questions are for us to internalize and reflect upon. With a group as large as I believe this one to be, I understand that you simply cannot afford to communicate frequently on an individual basis. That said, if you wish to have responses or feedback from us, I am more than willing to do so. Thank you for a great message.

— — —

The Goliath story is so true. Over the past few months we have had two tragedies in my family. In October my brother died, followed by the death of my father on October 30, 2013. I know that I am not the first person to loss a parent or brother, but what came to mind as I read your story was something I have come to understand since my divorce. That is faith is only as good as when you use it. It is when a parent dies, the giant attacks, sickness befalls you: then is when the rubber meets the road.

— — —

This is great stuff!! This is life-giving truth!! This is God's Truth!! It stirs my heart. Thank you for taking time to share. I can't wait till the next one comes.

— — —

What Men Said About Writing Their Stories for *What It Takes*

I feel like I have been cut in two. I pray that whatever appears on this page serves to point back to Him and shine His light on the lies of the deceiver.

— — —

While I had not previously committed my story to paper, I have gone over the details in my mind many times. I promised God that, given the opportunity, I would tell my story. Thanks for giving me the venue to write it down. God has been on my shoulder for almost 6 years now. Writing the story was a natural thing to do.

— — —

As with you, I am tempted to let regret creep in. "If only, I'd…" And then I remember that if I had not gone through my trial by fire, I could not have grown spiritually to where I am now (and I have so much more growing to do). I could have lived my entire life with, at best, a superficial relationship with God—at worst, eternally lost. I was so blessed to go through the trial although it has taken me a few years to see it that way. My relationship with God now is worth immeasurably more than anything I "lost."

— — —

In spite of the blessing of Grace and Forgiveness bestowed on me, even as I wrote I was reminded of how the deceiver never sleeps and tries to push doubt in the face of truth. I felt such a struggle of not being worthy of His love.

— — —

It's really tough to put into words on paper my story. There are so many details that I've left out and honestly, you're about the only person that knows all of those details anyway. I missed the deadline for submitting my story and I apologize but I still wanted you to have it. You can use my FULL name, date of birth, address, blood type I don't care. I'm proud of my story and I'll tell it to the world if they will listen.

Hope this is what you were looking for. Have a great weekend! My bride just walked in from work :)

~ ~ ~

Difficult. Reliving those days and condensing it into words was difficult. I was graphically reminded that as long as there is life, there is hope. Once I admitted to Jesus my iniquity and repented, really repented, Jesus stood up in my heart. Most of all, Jesus NEVER quit on me. NEVER!!

~ ~ ~

what it takes

Messages for Men Moved by God

LANCE COOPER

INLIGHT PUBLISHING
WORDS OF CLARITY

What It Takes
Messages for Men Moved by God

First Edition: July, 2016

ISBN: 978-0-9886139-4-2

Unless otherwise noted, Scripture in taken from the *Holy Bible: New International Version (NIV)*, copyright ©1973, 1978, 1984 by International Bible Society, used by permission

Also used: *New American Standard Bible* (NASB), © the Lockman Foundation, 1960, 1962, 1963, 1968, 1971, 1972, 1973, 1975, 1977. All rights reserved.

Also used: *New King James Version (NKJV)*, © 1979, 1980, 1982, Thomas Nelson, Inc., Publishers. All rights reserved.

Also used: *ESV® Bible* (The Holy Bible, English Standard Version®), copyright © 2001 by Crossway, a publishing ministry of Good News Publishers. Used by permission. All rights reserved.

Also used: *King James Version (KJV)*

Cover design: Jonathan Longnecker
Interior design: Adina Cucicov
Author's photograph: Lorelei Bryan, GentleTouchPortraits.com

Printed in the United States

InLight Publishing (words of clarity)

INLIGHT / PUBLISHING
WORDS OF CLARITY

To Important Men in My Life

Father—*Burnard Eugene Cooper*
Grandfathers—*Samuel Cooper and Grant Isaacs*
Brothers—*Marc Cooper and Mike Cooper*
Sons—*Matthew Cooper, Taylor Cooper, Ryan Cooper*
Grandsons—*Jon Cooper, Maxwell Cooper, Weston Cooper*
Nephews—*Gene Cooper, Marc Cooper, Brien Tolson, John Webb*

Men who have contributed to the leadership of the
Men's Gathering over the last decade and to the
thoughts and stories within *What It Takes.*

Dane Bledsoe
Roger Denny
David Duncan
Mark Dugger
Harlan Goan
Lyle Harris
Rodney Hightower
John James
Steve Suggs
Doug Tolson
Brian Westphalen
Judah Wilkins

Contents

Introduction...1

Take a walk. Explore. Discover manhood and what real men feel, think and do. Find out what makes them masculine. Start with us at the beginning. Face off the enemy. Battle with us with courage and honor. Ask God to go with you and to let you see His masterpiece—a man He has made for good works—you, the real you, the authentic man in you.

Join us. You will not be disappointed. God does not make mistakes. He makes all things new.

WEEK I: A MAN MOVED BY GOD....................................9
Bringing Stones Back to Life from Heaps of Rubble

Day 1   The Beginning of Man—Part I..........................13
Day 2   The Beginning of Man—Part II.........................17
Day 3   Woman...21
Day 4   Rebuilding Intimacy—Part I............................25

WEEK II: A MAN MOVED BY GOD...................................31
Restore to Me the Years

Day 5   Man Courage...35
Day 6   Man Work...39
Day 7   A Man's Very Best......................................45
Day 8   A Man's Heart...51

WEEK III: A MAN MOVED BY GOD..............................57
Putting Childish Ways Behind Me

Day 9   A Man's Talk...61
Day 10   A Man's Belief...67
Day 11   A Man's Desperate Decisions.................................73
Day 12   A Man's Signposts...79

WEEK IV: A MAN MOVED BY GOD...............................87
Could This Be the Christ?

Day 13   Men Stop the Cycle!...91
Day 14   The One Man Who Rescues.....................................97
Day 15   Men Who Struggle with God..................................103
Day 16   Men Can Be Trusted...109

WEEK V: A MAN MOVED BY GOD................................115
Acknowledge Him in All My Ways

Day 17   A Man's Faith Perseveres...................................119
Day 18   Men Chosen to Lead...125
Day 19   Men Who Know the Truth.....................................131
Day 20   Men Follow Jesus Wholeheartedly............................137

WEEK VI: A MAN MOVED BY GOD...............................145
That We Should Be Called Children of God

Day 21   Men Tell Stories...149
Day 22   Men Face Goliath...155
Day 23   A Man's Cave...161
Day 24   A Man's Big Decisions......................................167

WEEK VII: A MAN MOVED BY GOD..............................175
Acknowledge Him in All My Ways

Day 25   Mighty Men!..179
Day 26   Men Chase What Lasts!......................................187
Day 27   Rebuilding Intimacy—Part II!...............................193
Day 28   Men Soar Like Eagles!......................................199

WEEK VIII: A MAN MOVED BY GOD...205
Be Still and Know That He Is God

    Day 29 Men Avoid HER!...209
    Day 30 Men Forgive!...215
    Day 31 Men Love Children!.......................................221
    Day 32 Men Return Home!..227

WEEK IX: A MAN MOVED BY GOD..235
There Is Now No Condemnation

    Day 33 Transformation—Part I...................................241
    Day 34 The Transformation—Part II............................247
    Day 35 A Man's Confession....................................253
    Day 36 A Man's Idols...259

WEEK X: A MAN MOVED BY GOD...267
Who Shall Separate Us from the Love of Christ?

    Day 36 A Man's Story..271
    Day 38 A Man's Design..277
    Day 39 Love and Respect......................................287
    Day 40 A Man's Revelation....................................295

A MAN MOVED BY GOD...303
The Spirit Changes a Man

A MAN MOVED BY GOD...309
Father, Open My Eyes—Make Me Like You, Make Me Free!

MOVED BY GOD..315

Introduction

IT'S EARLY MORNING as the darkness lightens and the traffic increases on old Chapman Highway in Knoxville. People drive to work. I sit in a restaurant eating breakfast with a client, the rocks and streams of a forest-green land of trees and black bears beginning just a few miles away. The foggy mist is about to disappear and reveal the protected beauty of the Smokies outlined on the horizon.

I'm sitting with a CEO of a small business, and our conversation wanders from sales management to deeper matters. The topic turns to manhood just as the fog lifts from the Tennessee mountains. Something in the discussion captures my attention, and a few minutes into our eggs and biscuits he slides a book across the table—*Wild at Heart* by John Eldridge.

This moment and the many others after it are pieces of my decade-long journey with hundreds of men and multiple authors looking for something that has been lost—*what it means to be a man, an authentic man, a man moved by and made by God.*

COME WITH US

Take a walk. Explore. Discover manhood and what real men feel, think, and do. Find out what makes them masculine. Start with us at the beginning. Face off the enemy. Battle with us with courage and honor. Ask God to go with you and to let you see His master-piece—a man He has made for good works—you, the real you, the authentic man in you.

Join us. You will not be disappointed. God does not make mistakes. He makes all things new.

MANHOOD

It's another time, a hundred or even 1,000 years ago. Boys grow up at an early age in a wilderness of danger and challenge with fathers and other men who struggle to survive. The work of life begins early in the day and continues into the night. Wood is gathered, game is hunted, and land is cleared and farmed. Lions, wolves, weather, and snakes are daily enemies. Whether close at hand or an evil rising in a far away land, men face off against an imperfect world with courage, commitment, and sacrifice for the benefit of others, and for a few—the glory of God. They find their place in the line. They lead and protect others.

Today, men are confused. Sociologists like Michael Kimmel tell us that 22 million young men do not grow up until their late 20s (see his book _Guyland_). According to Mr. Kimmel's research, they sit in a Peter Pan world of sports, games, pornography, and binge drinking like an extended collegiate fraternity. Their world does not contain much commitment. It's also empty of direction or solid plans for dreams and futures.

Men find a twisted definition of masculinity streaming toward them from the media. Messages in movies and television tell everyone that men and women are the same and that women are able to best men physically, mentally, and socially. Men are babies. Men are weaklings. Men can't be trusted. Men ruin the lives of women. Stories in our entertainment world uplift women superheroes like in the cable mini-series *Nikita*, but downgrade masculine virtues and position men as irresponsible underachievers as in the Broadway play and Hollywood movie *Mamma Mia*.

THE CHANGES

The Industrial Revolution drew men off farms and into factories. The hours they used to spend working with their sons, and the natural mentoring and life lessons that occurred, were replaced. Instead, boys spent time alone with mom or with other guys and gals in an extended time of adolescence and education before beginning work to support themselves.

After World War II, the men of the "Greatest Generation" returned from war and kept silent about their battles. They went to work, but at home withdrew into a new media—T.V., and sat there watching with the horrors of the war seared deep within them. Communism was near and nuclear war was a possibility. Some of these men built underground, concrete bunkers, or they escaped into the recesses of alcohol or T.V. programming..

They also participated in great economic changes and the rise of suburban living. They gave their baby-boomer children too much, and instead of growing into responsible adults, boys remained boys sheltered from responsibility. Fascinating objects captured their hearts and minds—like '57 Chevrolets, marijuana, and Peter, Paul, and Mary's *Puff the Magic Dragon*.

Fast forward to the twenty-first century. The Internet weaves boys and girls into a new age tapestry of easy-to-access information. Multiple entertainment choices and alternative uses of time are available on handheld wireless devices. Teens can easily escape for hours in multiple directions and into a community of texts, pictures and videos. Video games woo kids into imaginary wars to commit murder, only to walk away without experiencing the real horrors associated with war.

Families split apart easily or never form. A boy lives with a girl and then another and another, and Adele sings into the torn spirits of female hearts. Drugs, alcohol, games, and multiple relationships with easy rules chase the blues away. We then wonder how it happens that a boy dressed in black brings a gun and terror into a school full of children.

Many young men do not see their biological father because he has left the family. Some dads are present in the flesh yet emotionally absent, lost in their headphones and the matrix around them. As David Popenoe writes in *Life Without Father*, absent fathers create aimless boys who go through school with low effort, no ambition and bad grades. They enter their 20s not knowing who they are as men or what it takes to make a dream real. Mr. Kimmel gives some hope and states that many "guys" know that something isn't right. But, when they look around, they can't see the model of a real man.

It's sad to see some of them firmly sown as a tight knot into the "net." They do not realize the passage of time until the losses in their lives begin to give them grey hair in old alleys and a Bordeaux of spilled manhood without any real traction.

In some families where moms and dads do pay attention, we often see "helicopter parenting." These parents hover over their children, orchestrating every moment as a protective cover for their lives. As a result, boys do not learn the reality of struggles and hard choices as they attempt to win a prize. They do not learn the meaning of sacrifice. They do not learn the hard lessons surrounding goal achievement. In her book *Mindset*, Dr. Carol Drevick describes how boys learn to believe that success should be easy and that trophies are earned by just showing up. If achieving results gets hard and long, they quit. It gets tough and they give up. If they can't be perfect, they don't try, and so real life and its necessary commitments evades them.

SPIRITUAL EMPTINESS

Men live with a conscience and behave according to what is written on their hearts. While it's evident that love, peace, patience and self-control are good virtues, some men avoid these evidential truths and behave as if they do not exist. Others, while having them at some level, do so in a self-powered approach. They walk alone and depend upon themselves or those around them for defining truth.

There's a hole in the heart of a man not connected to the God who made him. Even if he possesses love or joy or peace or patience to some degree, he does not acknowledge the source. And that leaves uncertainty now or as he approaches the end of life. Questions emerge: "What's missing? What's the point of it all?"

Today, something's missing in a man's identity. He walks through life trying to find himself and his manhood in dark places, in binge drinking, in his 401K, his job or his achievements. For a few, women become THE adventure, but more and more women, including virtual ones, never seem to help him find himself.

Men walk burdened with things that weigh them down as they attempt to use them to control life. This creates fear, then anger. They look in all the wrong places for their significance and their manhood, and they escape into a Stephen King world of *Needful Things*—all of which bring harm and destruction to themselves and those around them.

Christian men are not immune. Many of them are in the clutches of secularism and their outward behaviors look the same to those who do not believe in God—just as many divorces, just as much pornography and violence. The research arm of the Barna Group finds that only 19 percent of Christians believe in the following fundamental truths of Christianity:

§ Moral truth is absolute and unaffected by circumstances
§ The Bible is accurate in all the principles it teaches
§ Satan is a real force

§ It is impossible to earn your way into heaven through good behavior
§ Jesus Christ lived a sinless life while on earth
§ God is an all-powerful, all-knowing creator of the uerse who still rules today.

MEN MOVED BY GOD

In the last 10 years, I have seen hundreds of men encounter the living God in their lives. I've watched His changes occur in them and I've seen the effect on their work, their friends and their families. Young and old—age hasn't mattered. Men have learned who they are as men. No longer confused, they have found their hearts healed by Jesus.

This book starts with Genesis, the first book of the Bible, and will take you on a man's path of discovery. I designed the book as an ten week study for a group of men to experience together. Each week begins with a man's story and is followed by 4 messages with study questions to help you explore God's will for your life. There are 40 days of messages with questions and actions for men willing to look for a relationship or deeper connection with God. In the same amount of time, Jesus was led by the Spirit of His Father into the desert to fast and pray and grow as a man. In that barren landscape, hungry, thirsty and alone, He faced a powerful and dangerous enemy. Please expect Jesus to show up as you study, and for Jesus and His Father and the Spirit of God to intersect with your life. If you do, I do not promise you an easy road, but I do promise you a better one.

Twelve men have allowed me to include their stories in this book. These stories were difficult for them to write, but they were written so that you might be encouraged in your own journey. Jesus changed these men forever, and the change was good—*very good.*

MY DESIRES FOR YOU

I want you to grow stronger—to take a journey into authentic manhood with the Spirit of God. I want you to find yourself in Him. I want you to be able to look at someone and boldly proclaim how you're different because of Jesus and His work upon your heart. I want you to know that you're a better man and that you will continue to grow stronger every day as you connect yourself to the God who made you. I want you to know how to treat women and children in ways that are strong and loving and protective. I want you to know, *"You Have What It Takes!"*

" ... Can they bring the stones back
to life from those heaps of rubble?"

Nehemiah 4:2

A Man Moved by God

Bringing Stones Back to Life from Heaps of Rubble

IN JULY OF 2002, that was a pretty good description of my life....a heap of rubble. I was at the bottom. My third marriage almost cost me my life, literally. I lost my 182-acre ranch, my horses, my tractor and all the awards I had accumulated in life. I had no home to call my own, no car and no job. I only had the clothes on my back and a brother in North Carolina who was willing to give me a place to sleep. Make no mistake about it, where I found myself in July 2002 did not come suddenly. It happened slowly over a period of many years and culminated with a life-changing event in 1996. Like the Titanic's impact on an iceberg, my daughter's sudden death on October 3, 1996 was the beginning of the end for me. Pam was 25. From that moment, until I finally sank in July 2002, it was a downward spiral. Here is the short version of what happened.

Elise and I were forced to quit high school because she was pregnant with our son, Lex. Elise became ill and I took custody of Lex and later remarried for nearly 30 years. Elise also remarried for 34 years but she never saw Lex until 40 years later.

As a very young father, I heard the Gospel and surrendered my life to Jesus. My life changed. I had a walk with Jesus. God blessed and directed me in my labors for more than 30 years. I started Christian schools, pastored two churches, started a new business, was elected and reelected as a County Judge, served as a District County Administrator and worked for both the Montana and Tennessee Supreme Courts as a Deputy Director. Looking at my life one would probably say I was successful. But if you could have examined my heart, you would have seen a desperate man in danger of heart failure.

Proverbs 4 includes a lot of great advice about wisdom and success, but in verse 23 it says, "*Above all else,* guard your heart, for everything you do flows from it." I learned the hard way that the most important thing was to "guard my heart". I had guarded my career with each new opportunity, but I had failed to guard my heart, and piece-by-piece, my heart was being eaten away. The communion I had known with God began to slip. The eternal things that were once important slowly gave way to other stuff—women, in particular.

My "heap of rubble" was the result of years of internal erosion much like the damage termites do to a home. Everything looked good on the outside. The paint was still intact, the walls looked okay, but down inside the "home" where human eyes cannot see, the infrastructure was slowly being eaten away.

When Pam was killed, I had no infrastructure to hold me, and I collapsed. I propped myself up temporarily with alcohol, sex, pride and working harder, but just like the Titanic, I was headed for the bottom. And that is where I ended up.

But that is not the end of my story…….

When I collapsed in a "heap of rubble" and cried out for God's mercy and forgiveness, I recognized a voice and a presence I had not heard or felt for many years. The parable of the lost son in Luke 15 has great significance to me today. Jesus met me with forgiveness, not condemnation. He did not rub my nose in my failures or make me feel second rate. I was truly repentant, and Jesus fully embraced me just like the parable in Luke 15.

If this story were fiction, I could pen a happy ending in a few short paragraphs. Not so here, because these things really happened. The road back took time, tears, forgiveness, hard work, new decisions, determination and humility, and it was often difficult. Did I say humility? God was so good to lead me and make me feel wanted. During this time, I began to understand termites and how I had allowed them to steal my power, my manhood and most of all, my relationship with God.

However, in 2005, God performed a miracle! My Savior reunited me with my first wife, Elise, the mother of our son. In the Fall of 2005, Elise and I traveled to San Antonio and she met Lex and his family for the first time in more than 40 years. Indescribable! Only God could do this. I am a blessed man. I would love to tell you more, but time and space will not permit.

I will say this—David killed a giant, but it was the "termites" working in his heart that took him out. He failed to "guard his heart". I think American men have been trained to look for and slay the giants, the big things—graduation from a hip school, an admired career, the ultimate income, the right woman, and so on. But it is the termites—pride, lust, greed, hatred, grudges, anger, coldness to God, etc.—that are hidden down deep in our hearts that erode our lives. And then when the storm comes, we collapse because there is no infrastructure—Jesus.

Jesus is the only one who can heal the heart. Jesus is the only one who can get rid of the termites. Jesus is the only one who can "bring the stones back to life from those heaps of rubble."

If you are alive and can read what I have written, it is never too late to find your walk with Jesus. Never too late! There is no other way.

The Beginning of Man—Part I

THIS IS THE history of the heavens and of the earth when they were created in the day that the Lord created the heavens and the earth before any plant of the field was in the earth and there was no man to till the ground, but a mist went up from the earth and watered the whole face of the ground. And the Lord God formed man of the dust of the ground and breathed into his nostrils the breath of life; and man became a living being.

The Lord God planted a garden, and there He put the man He had formed. And the trees and plants around him were pleasant, stunning to see and good for food. The Lord God took the man and put him in the Garden of Eden to tend it and to keep it. (Gen. 2: 4-7; 8-9; 15 NKJV)

Today, the familiar sounds of the earth waking around us with cars and flying machines remind us that things are in movement. Deep in our hearts, yet unmet in glorious form and begging for release, our spirit reminds us of our purpose and of the time when man was free to roam in a world just forming. Then, we were perfect, unblemished and good. As our God walked with us, we took care of the parts of the creation that fed us. We kept it.

Today, this day, work well. Start the day talking to God. Face this broken world and your imperfect, blemished heart with the King of kings—Jesus. Look for His intersection with your life—today.

Love God. Love others. Grow stronger. Learn new things. Fight. Be vigilant. Take courage in the Lord God. He loves you.

Just take a look at Jesus. He is good. He will make you into a new creation and He will keep shaping you through every struggle, trial, and victory. Win today. Be successful today. Fight for an inch of new ground today. Do your best for the benefit of others and for the glory of the Lord God, and till the ground you've been given.

He will fill in the furrows you miss when you let him push you along in a righteous direction. Then, today, what you do WILL be GOOD.

THE BEGINNING OF MAN—PART I
(your thoughts and actions)

Read Genesis 1-2:19. Picture the days before the fall of man. What was it like?

_____

_____

_____

_____

_____

Look at your life. What is most imperfect (not good) about it? Don't settle on your initial answer. Close your eyes and allow yourself to look at how you live. Be honest. Ask God to reveal your deepest need for Him. When you think you know what it is, write it down.

_____

_____

_____

_____

_____

How does that part of your life affect God?

_____

_____

_____

_____

_____

How does it affect others?

_____

_____

_____

_____

_____

_____

How does it affect you?

_____

_____

_____

_____

_____

_____

Stop right now and tell God about your sorrow. Ask for His forgiveness. Ask for Him to move you to be a better man.

_____

_____

_____

_____

_____

_____

As you continue with each of the forty messages, look for God's movement in your life and celebrate the changes that occur—what He teaches you and how He changes you. Find someone you can talk to about what He is doing for you. Talk to them. Tell them.

DAY 2

The Beginning of Man—Part II

THEN GOD SAID, "Let us make man in Our image, according to Our likeness: let them have dominion over the fish of the sea, over the birds of the air, and over the cattle, over all the earth and over every creeping thing that creeps on the earth" ... so God created man in His own image, in the image of God He created him; male and female He created them. Then, God blessed them, and God said to them, "Be fruitful and multiply; fill the earth and subdue it; have dominion over the fish of the sea, over the birds of the air, and over every living thing that moves on the earth.

Then God saw everything He had made and indeed it was very good.

(Gen. 1:26, 28, 31 NKJV)

We are made in God's image, in the image of Jesus, in the image of the Holy Spirit—in THEIR likeness. Wow!

We have dominion over the earth. What a responsibility!

We were made very good... VERY GOOD!

Yet today we fight the tendencies and habits that wage war in our hearts in a uerse subjected to frustration and decay. We fight to remember who we are as we exist within the groaning of the whole creation: CHILDREN OF GOD!

We fight to keep ourselves doing the right things. We fight to protect those in our care. We fight for the things that we learn or know are true. We fight for our relationship with God and for our friends and family, and we fight against the forces that would set us apart. We do this with His power and with His blessing and with His strength and with His love for us.

He knows we are very good when He sees the Son in our hearts—making us new, making us free again, making us His.

THE BEGINNING OF MAN—PART II

(your thoughts and actions)

What do you think it means to be created in the image of God—according to His likeness?

_____

_____

_____

_____

_____

_____

Look up the word "good." What does it mean? Now, write down what it's like to be made "very good.'

_____

_____

_____

_____

_____

_____

Read Ephesians 2:1-10. What does God say to you through the words of the apostle Paul?

_____

_____

_____

_____

_____

_____

God sent His Son, Jesus, to bring us back to Him and to give us a new beginning—a rebirth. What does Peter say that Jesus gives us a new birth into? (1 Peter 1:3)

_____

_____

_____

_____

_____

_____

Ask God to continue the work He began in you yesterday. Ask Him to increase your faith and hope in Him.

_____

_____

_____

_____

_____

_____

Go out and work today for Him. Make life better for those you serve, lead and protect.

Remember, "For we are God's workmanship, created in Christ Jesus to do good works, which God prepared in advance for us to do" (Eph. 2:10). And, "For God did not give us a spirit of timidity, but a spirit of power, of love and of self-discipline" (2 Tim. 1: 7).

Take on the day with HIM!

DAY 3

Woman

THE LORD GOD said, "It is not good for the man to be alone. I will make a helper suitable for him."

Now the LORD God had formed out of the ground all the beasts of the field and all the birds of the air. He brought them to the man to see what he would name them; and, whatever the man called each living creature, that was its name. So the man gave names to all the livestock, the birds of the air and all the beasts of the field.

But for Adam no suitable helper was found. So the LORD God caused the man to fall into a deep sleep; and while he was sleeping, he took one of the man's ribs and closed up the place with flesh. Then the LORD God made a woman from the rib he had taken out of the man, and he brought her to the man.

The man said, "This is now bone of my bones and flesh of my flesh; she shall be called 'woman,' for she was taken out of man."

For this reason a man will leave his father and mother and be united to his wife, and they will become one flesh. The man and his wife were both naked, and they felt no shame.

(Gen. 2:18-25)

It's not good for a man to be alone. He gets confused. He gets in trouble. The idols he worships hinder his peace in life. He finds no enjoyment in his work. It's all toil. It's work and it has no lasting purpose. It's actually a miserable Scrooge-like existence. If he gets in trouble, there's no one to help him.

There was a man all alone; he had neither son nor brother.

There was no end to his toil, yet his eyes were not content with his wealth.

"For whom am I toiling," he asked, "and why am I depriving myself of enjoyment?"

This too is meaningless—a miserable business!

Two are better than one, because they have a good return for their work:

If one falls down, his friend can help him up.

But pity the man who falls and has no one to help him up!

Also, if two lie down together, they will keep warm. But how can one keep warm alone?

Though one may be overpowered, two can defend themselves.

A cord of three strands is not quickly broken. (Eccl. 4: 8-12)

It's important to have two or more close friends. It especially helps our hearts if we grow into knowing our brides as our best friends—even starting out that way from the beginning, though many of us do not. She can be the person with whom we are most intimate. As we struggle together against the forces that buffet our lives, we help each other and find joy and hope and love as we work and fight within a crumbling world. Her intuition saves us. Our might protects her. And, as time passes, the transparent honesty that passes between us is emptied of anger and passivity and filled with delight in each other's presence, without shame.

WOMAN
(your thoughts and actions)

Are you lonely? Simple question, but important. Are you lonely? Yes or no?

_____

_____

_____

_____

_____

If you are married, do you see your wife as now "bone of your bones and flesh of your flesh?" The right answer for many men is no, because intimacy between man and woman was shattered by sin. But we can work hard to rebuild this lost intimacy of the ages. What sins, thoughts, or behaviors lie between you and your bride? What activities do you rationalize as OK that keep you from working at strengthening relationships? As you pray and think about this lesson, look for God's movement in your life. Answer this question, what grand purpose or simple action can make you better as a husband or a friend—today?

_____

_____

_____

_____

_____

If you are single or married, ask God where you can serve as a companion to others. With whom can you do recreational activities with and enjoy the influence of their company because it helps you grow as a child of God? Where can you give yourself in friendship? How can you share your faith with others? Whom can you stand beside?

_____

_____

_____

_____

_____

_____

Remember this. We can befriend anyone in the world as long as that friendship does not lead to shared values apart from and against God and His commands for our lives. A healthy man will spend many hours with other men of God.

Rebuilding Intimacy—Part I

NOW THE SERPENT was more crafty than any of the wild animals the LORD God had made. He said to the woman, "Did God really say, 'You must not eat from any tree in the garden'?"

The woman said to the serpent, "We may eat fruit from the trees in the garden, but God did say, 'You must not eat fruit from the tree that is in the middle of the garden, and you must not touch it, or you will die.'"

"You will not surely die," the serpent said to the woman. "For God knows that when you eat of it your eyes will be opened, and you will be like God, knowing good and evil."

When the woman saw that the fruit of the tree was good for food and pleasing to the eye, and also desirable for gaining wisdom, she took some and ate it. She also gave some to her husband, who was with her, and he ate it. Then the eyes of both of them were opened, and they realized they were naked; so they sewed fig leaves together and made coverings for themselves.

Then the man and his wife heard the sound of the LORD God as he was walking in the garden in the cool of the day, and they hid from the LORD God among the trees of the garden.

(Gen. 3:1-8)

God is good. He made the creation and us very "good." He can be trusted even though men wonder at times how God can allow nature or people to hurt other people, our family, or even hurt us.

We do not understand the forces of heaven in conflict with us and aligned against us.

We do see Jesus on the cross dying for each one of us, even when men hurt each other. By faith in Jesus, we know God loves us.

Every day, we hear the lies woven into the fabric of the world—drawing us, blinding us, teaching us about evil, decay, and spiritual death. Cars that will soothe our spirits. Drinks that will make us manly. Money that will give us control. Women who will give us significance. Knowledge that will make us wise in our selves. Empty vessels of promises that do not satisfy but blind us to a godly life of peace, joy, and hope. Our anxieties and fears in these broken cisterns and frantic lives show us where we place our trust.

We remember His words. So, when He says to do something, it's good for us to do it—very good. We guard our thoughts and take them captive. We speak into the world with His directives and with new behaviors, and we fight with the Spirit's weapons: love, joy, peace, patience, kindness, goodness, faithfulness, gentleness, and self-control. We act in these things with aggression. We remove ourselves from hidden places. We believe Him. We trust Him. We walk with Him, AGAIN!

REBUILDING INTIMACY—PART I
(your thoughts and actions)

A man's courage affects his intimacy with God and with his bride. When a man hides from the battles of spiritual development, he avoids the things that bring the forces of God's kingdom into his heart. Where can you throw your heart and mind and learn how to grow as a man of God?

_____

_____

_____

_____

_____

In what area of your life are you silent with God—an area that He sees and one in which you need His leading? Write it down and offer it to him in prayer,

_____

_____

_____

_____

_____

What do you care about more than intimacy with your bride or intimacy with Jesus? If not in God, where do you place your trust?

_____

_____

_____

_____

_____

If you stopped posing and hiding and keeping yourself from being real with God, what would be revealed first as your deepest need? Please remain silent and think about this now. Write down your answer.

_____

_____

_____

_____

_____

_____

As you begin this day, continue praying and thinking about "your greatest need." Offer this to God in prayer. Jesus asked, "What do you want me to do for you?" The blind man replied, "Lord, I want to see" (Luke 18:41).

"I will restore to you the years that the swarming locust has eaten..."

Joel 2:25 NKJV

A Man Moved by God

Restore to Me the Years

I THOUGHT THE story would get easier with the telling, but it has not. Because of the time elapsed—34 years—the original sting is not there, but regret rears its ugly head on occasion! It keeps me on my toes and sensitive to external distractions that Satan would love to use to tear me down again. I never cease to awe in the glorious saving power of the risen Savior.

I do not have to strive to "be good" on my own. I have proven time and time again that this is impossible. I still fail at times and have pity parties that show my lack of trust in Jesus, but they are fewer and further between.

I was forced into the limelight at the age of 14. This was the junior-age Sunday school department of my home church in Chattanooga. One Sunday morning the superintendent called me to the front and told me to lead singing! I had never done that before, nor had I ever been in front of people as a song leader. I didn't have any more sense than to just go up there and "wing" it.

My parents had served this church for 30 years at that time and our family was highly respected. Everything I did was praised, not because it was all that good, but because I was a Harris.

I enjoyed music and sang regularly in area churches and with the local opera association while I was in high school. When I entered college, it seemed reasonable to major in music. I continued to sing and conduct and served a local church as music director the last two years of school.

For the next 10 years, the churches I served grew bigger and opportunities to be in the limelight abounded. By then, I had held several music seminars on performance and platform work in distribution around the country. I had also traveled with Jack Van Impe to do two citywide evangelistic crusades.

I really did not need a relationship with Christ because I had the admiration of the public. I was working long hours at the last church I served from 1976 through 1980. I had no days off and the stress level was fairly intense.

While married, I began a daily conversation with a worker in the cafeteria of our Christian school that led to more and more intimate conversations until I was stopping by her house on the way home after "working late". Even after my sexual immorality was exposed and I resigned, there were still a couple of churches that wanted to hire me. Because of the national presence of the church, the pastor thought it best to cover up the issue rather than go public. I knew that my career as a professional Christian musician was over, but I was not sure of the future.

My wife is my hero, exemplifying Christ in every aspect of restoration, forgiveness and the rebuilding of trust. We moved to Knoxville in 1981 in need of a grace experience which none of the churches we served or grew up in offered. We found that at Berean

Bible Church. They were so patient, loving and understanding of us and walked with us on this journey of recovery.

Today, volunteer ministries abound and Christ has proven Himself faithful in allowing us to minister and serve those who are hurting. We have shared our story twice before our church and have had affirming conversations with couples with similar situations in their past.

Seeing God work in other men challenges me on, and I look to Christ to "restore to me the years that the swarming locust has eaten" (Joel 2:25 ESV).

With Jesus I have what it takes, and so do you!

DAY 5

Man Courage

BUT THE LORD God called to the man, "Where are you?"

He answered, "I heard you in the garden, and I was afraid because I was naked; so I hid."

And He said, "Who told you that you were naked? Have you eaten from the tree that I commanded you not to eat from?"

The man said, "The woman you put here with me–she gave me some fruit from the tree, and I ate it."

Then the LORD God said to the woman, "What is this you have done?" The woman said, "The serpent deceived me, and I ate."

(Gen 3:9-13)

Where are you? No really, where are you REALLY? When you look deep inside your spirit, are you afraid? Are you hiding? Are you using things to control your life and perhaps those around you? Are you taking things to the extreme? Are you into things that give you pleasure to the extent that they take you away from responsibilities and commitments? Do you crave recognition and look for significance, even from bodies in a magazine or on the Internet or at the office or at home? Do you allow your manhood to drain onto the ground in anger, passivity, or nakedness?

No! You live as a Prince of the KING—a child of God—a warrior. Everyday you stride into a broken world to wage war in a spiritual battle. You might be a doctor, an engineer, a salesman, or a laborer, but you remember Jesus as He urges you on, "It is I, take courage. Don't be afraid." "Take up your cross and follow me."

You protect your family. You protect people at work. You receive your pleasure and comfort and significance from battles won in the hearts of those around you. You avoid meaningless talk and you listen for words that give life, and you hear them without distortion. You keep yourself pure by continuing to listen to the KING as you walk with Him daily. And, when you hear the siren, the money, or the pleasure telling you it's OK, you tell them NO! You receive hope and joy and love won in a struggle to make things better, and you are at peace.

You hold on to your faith, and if you fall, you get up! If you fall, you get up! If you fall, you get up and STAND again!

Today, this morning, this afternoon, this evening, you will...

"Be on your guard; stand firm in the faith; be men of courage; be strong."

So, remember, "Do not be afraid; do not be discouraged; be strong and courageous (Joshua 10:25)."

"Do not turn aside to the right or to the left (Deut. 5:32)." Stay focused on THE way.

Where are YOU? Today?

You stand in front of those you protect, without shame, living a meaningful life, forgiven and bold, following Christ!

~ ~ ~

MAN COURAGE
(your thoughts and actions)

Where are you? When you look deep inside, are you afraid? Are you hiding with things that comfort you, give you control or give you significance? Are you using things to control your life and perhaps those around you? Are you taking things to the extreme? What do you need to let go of?

_____

_____

_____

_____

_____

_____

Are you into things that give you pleasure to the extent that they take you away from responsibilities and commitments? Do you crave recognition and look for significance, even from bodies in a magazine or on the Internet or at the office or at home? Do you allow your manhood to drain onto the ground in anger, passivity or nakedness? What do you need to walk away from that does not strengthen your manhood as God's son?

_____

_____

_____

_____

_____

_____

Ask God right now in prayer to reveal what you hold onto and grasp other than Him. What is your needful thing?

_____

_____

_____

_____

_____

_____

Who are you? If Jesus asked you, "Who are you?" what would you say? How would you identify yourself beyond your name?

_____

_____

_____

_____

_____

_____

How can you approach today without hiding and stand in courage as a man of God?

_____

_____

_____

_____

_____

God only wants us to hold onto a few things in our hearts: His instruction, His love, the salvation of His Son, and faith and hope in Him.

DAY 6

Man Work

TO ADAM HE said, "Because you listened to your wife and ate from the tree about which I commanded you, 'You must not eat of it,'

Cursed is the ground because of you; through painful toil you will eat of it all the days of your life.

It will produce thorns and thistles for you, and you will eat the plants of the field. By the sweat of your brow you will eat your food until you return to the ground, since from it you were taken; for dust you are and to dust you will return."

(Gen 3:17-19)

Men work the land into waiting furrows of earth ready for seed. Rocks get in the way. The ground resists then gives way—resists then gives way. The sun brings heat to the work and the backs of laborers. Water pours from bodies as equipment moves to create a place for seeds and life. In the weeks ahead, men beat back the weeds and hope for rain and sun in just the right mixture—sometimes crying out for water or light.

For months, the work continues until time for harvest. The ground is turned again and the produce picked and carried off for packing where men move crates from truck to railroad to ship to truck to store. A salesman walks through door after door beating through the frowns and pavement for a sale, and then takes the money and walks into the same store to buy an apple and food for the week ahead. People sit at desks and bend over file cabinets pushing paper or email or talking on phones all over the world just to buy some food, clothing, shelter and comfort.

Toys, gadgets, lawnmowers, cell phones, computers, homes, automobiles and iPads occupy our minds and elevate our anxiety with additional breakdown, maintenance, and desire for more. Add that to our losses in relationships, our sins and insatiable need for comfort, significance and control, and maybe we understand how cursed the ground is compared to a time long ago before our knowledge of good and evil.

In toil and pain, thorns and thistles, we work to make ourselves feel good, safe, powerful or known by man. If we accept this, we die lonely with our music buried deep within us.

～ ～ ～

Men, stop the cycle, and as Paul says, "godless chatter!" Accept that life is difficult. Get up and face the day with Jesus and a newly forming spirit that is powerful beyond words and very ABLE to stand and fight. From a wheelchair or poverty, you have what it takes. Jesus!

Because of Him, "Consider it pure joy when you face trials of many kinds, because you know that the testing of your faith develops perseverance. Perseverance must finish its work so that you may be mature and complete, not lacking anything" (James 1: 2-4).

So, find joy in the toil of hard work! Find joy in beating back the obstacles. Find beauty underneath what was broken or undeveloped. Do this with God and with the hearts of other valiant men.

Without waiting for just the right conditions, plant and reap. Your faith will show itself in the tapestry of your work—the latter a product of the former: faith-producing work that pleases the King of kings.

Solomon declared, "Whatever your hand finds to do, <u>do it with all your might,</u> for in the grave, where you are going, there is neither working nor planning nor knowledge nor wisdom," and, "A fool's work wearies him" (Eccl. 9:10; 10:15).

Work at loving God and loving others in all you do.

Now, today is a new day! Get up! Be strong in the grace that is in Christ Jesus. Endure hardship like a good soldier in Him and with a spirit of love, power, and self-discipline.

～ ～ ～

MAN WORK
(your thoughts and actions)

Please describe what you think about work.

Describe the work tasks you love to do. What tasks do you not like doing? What's the difference?

Were you taught that work should be easy, or were you taught that work and achievement require sweat and sacrifice and toil in hard conditions? How would either of these teachings affect you today, especially as you experience the difficulty and frustrations of work or the creation of new habits?

What if you work to please others? What might happen with this approach?

_____

_____

_____

_____

_____

_____

What is the best way to approach work each day?

_____

_____

_____

_____

_____

We will work until we die. It's healthy for men to approach life's challenges in partnership with God. Our joy increases as His Spirit leads us into and through the challenges of the day. He gives us victories as we work for His glory and the benefit of those around us.

Work to please Him and Him alone. Everything else will find its rightful place.

DAY 7

A Man's Very Best

ADAM LAY WITH his wife Eve, and she became pregnant and gave birth to Cain. She said, "With the help of the LORD I have brought forth a man." Later she gave birth to his brother Abel. Now Abel kept flocks, and Cain worked the soil.

In the course of time, Cain brought some of the fruits of the soil as an offering to the LORD. But Abel brought fat portions from some of the firstborn of his flock. The LORD looked with favor on Abel and his offering, but on Cain and his offering he did not look with favor. So Cain was very angry, and his face was downcast.

Then the LORD said to Cain, "Why are you angry? Why is your face downcast? If you do what is right, will you not be accepted? But if you do not do what is right, sin is crouching at your door; it desires to have you, but you must master it."

(Gen. 4:1-7)

Have you ever held back at work, at home, or in your relationship with God? Who hasn't? I have more times than I know. Have you ever thought of that as a condition of your heart?

Today, I watch men work, lead their families, and live out their lives for Jesus with one foot on the brake. They lean back in spiritual apathy. They don't commit. They hold back. They keep the best for themselves and use it to make life comfortable. They sit in passivity without godly goals or strong direction. They take the gifts God gave them and escape to safe places where time passes, and they miss the favor of the Lord.

When their self-directed actions and thoughts fail to bring meaning and joy, they sink deeper into their false pleasures, or they become angry and downcast. The same continued sins seem to wait on them like crouching tigers.

I see other men walking into the uncertain darkness, then falling to their knees and asking the Lord for strength to overcome. These men rush to hear and learn about the good news of Christ and the power of His life on the world around them. They find freedom in His forgiveness extended to everyone who believes in Him. They find their habits at war now with the Spirit that, in the crucible of conscience, faith and effort, changes them into His likeness. Love, joy, peace, patience and other spiritual powers of action and discernment mold their lives through the Spirit of God.

Gratitude overwhelms them. His majesty captures their hearts as they sense His power in the creation around them and in them. They again learn to walk with God like in the beginning. In that walk, anger lessens as their souls lean into faith and hope in the Lord. With His power, they master sin instead of letting it control them, and they become a slave to doing more and more good. Even in despair and great odds they cling to faith.

These are dangerous men to the forces of evil. These are forceful men advancing the kingdom of heaven. In many of these men, nothing seems to indicate by outward appearance the weight of their might and power. Yet, others see the favor of the Lord upon them.

You can change. You can grow. You can sacrifice what you've been given—your talents or your possessions. You can give food and clothes to feed or care for someone else. You can lead your family into a deeper relationship with God. You can be better.

You can endure difficult times and impossible conditions. You can make a difference in this world. You can give your best for the benefit of others and for the magnificence of the Lord's gift to you in Jesus, and you can do this because you love Him.

He loves you. Today, give Him your very best. Change the world.

A MAN'S VERY BEST
(your thoughts and actions)

Are you a part of changing the world? Do you get up each morning realizing your place in the adventure of all adventures?

What is the condition of your heart toward God during the day, at home, or when you enter a church? Describe its condition these days.

What would your life look like if you gave the best of you to God's work?

How would that change how people see you at work?

_____

_____

_____

_____

_____

_____

How would that change the impact you would have on your friends and family?

_____

_____

_____

_____

_____

_____

Be "all in." Give your whole heart to Jesus. This simple and profound beginning will put you at the front of the battle and in the heart of the adventure. It will take you into the darkness with the light of Christ and the power of God. It will make you fully alive, vulnerable to Him and impenetrable to the forces of evil. And though you may be knocked down and fall, as a righteous man you will rise again and again and again.

A Man's Heart

THE LORD SAW how great man's wickedness on the earth had become, and that every inclination of the thoughts of his heart was only evil all the time. The LORD was grieved that he had made man on the earth, and his heart was filled with pain. So the LORD said, "I will wipe mankind, whom I have created, from the face of the earth-men and animals, and creatures that move along the ground, and birds of the air-for I am grieved that I have made them."

But Noah found favor in the eyes of the LORD. This is the account of Noah. Noah was a righteous man, blameless among the people of his time, and he walked with God.

(Gen. 6:5-9)

What does God see when he looks at your life and at the lives of those from whom you seek wisdom—especially when He looks in the secret places, the dark places, the places you keep for yourself apart from Him?

What does He see when He looks at our home, our city, our county, our state, our government, and the world? How do we display the inclinations of our hearts in newspapers, talk radio, or in our chatter together? What about in the secret places? Do we grieve Him as he watches us? Is His heart filled with pain?

A long time ago, every inclination of the hearts of men were evil all the time (Gen. 6:5) and God decided to destroy mankind. One man, Noah, found favor in the eyes of the Lord. Today, one man saves us again—Jesus, fully man, fully God. Today, the final agreement between God and man completes itself. In whose boat will you ride out the days ahead?

When Jesus fills your heart, He reveals every secret place by fire (his testing) and light (his rebirth). He teaches you to walk again with God and He sees you as He did Adam in the beginning, pure, innocent, and free.

Because of our faith, Jesus graces us with forgiveness and righteousness, even though we deserve death and destruction. Rather than destroy us, he took the life of His only Son and allowed Him to die for us on a cross over 2000 years ago. Since God cannot be in the presence of sin, His son took on our sins, suffered and died in our place.

Wow. He loves us that much. It's an old, old story that always moves those who hear it in their hearts and respond to the prompting of His Spirit.

So, work every day to find favor in the eyes of the Lord. Find righteousness through your belief in Jesus. Work out your faith with trembling at His cost and sacrifice, with overwhelming gratitude and reverential respect. Look at those around you and love them more and more and more as you find your place once again walking with the Father of us all.

Desire for God to look at you through His Son's eyes and see something today that makes Him smile and then laugh, and the sunshine of His laughter might just save many others around you.

Do this. Be blameless. Walk with Him. People need your love. They need His love.

God will use the glorious YOU to save the world through His Son.

———

A MAN'S HEART
(your thoughts and actions)

Do you believe that you find favor in the eyes of the Lord?

_____

_____

_____

_____

_____

_____

How is Noah described?

_____

_____

_____

_____

_____

What would need to change in your life for you to find favor in the eyes of the Lord?

_____

_____

_____

_____

_____

What does Solomon remind us of in this proverb? (Prov. 4:23)

_____

_____

_____

_____

_____

_____

Please read Philippians 4:4-8. Write down what Paul says will guard your heart and mind in Christ Jesus.

_____

_____

_____

_____

_____

Those who give their lives to Christ Jesus already have the favor of God, and the evidence of this is Jesus hanging on a cross for the sins of each man. Each day we live our lives in awesome respect of the KING of kings, and in honor we give our lives to Him and in service to those around us.

"When I was a child, I talked like a child, I thought like a child, I reasoned like a child. When I became a man, I put childish ways behind me."

1 Corinthians 13:11

A Man Moved by God

Putting Childish Ways Behind Me

IT WAS DECEMBER 19, 2013 around 9:00 a.m. CST. I was sitting in my car outside one of our retail stores in Clarksville, Tennessee when I received a phone call. I immediately dropped everything I was doing and answered with "Hello." I'll never forget that day for it was cold and rainy outside, which happened to mirror the feelings in my heart. I was broken...

I didn't grow up in the Church but was christened Methodist as a baby. The few memories I have of the Church are so blurry now that I almost can't even make them out. My story isn't that of a kid who grew up on the streets or was from a "broken home." I have a great family full of love, but like most families, we had our own set of challenges. I had everything I ever needed and most of what I wanted. However, things started to change a few years ago, and being the independent, type A, ADD dynamo that I am, I was going to figure it out on my own. I didn't need anybody or anything.

Some things happened in my life that I was very angry about, and I began to behave very differently. I come from a long line of alcoholics—generation after generation of alcoholics. Heck, my great grandfather used to run moonshine for Al Capone back in the day. It was in my blood; it was who I was. The past three years had been exceptionally difficult for me so I turned to the bottle as a coping mechanism, and self-medicated. I made some choices, did some things and said things I wasn't proud of, but most of all, I hated who I had become. I literally felt like I was dying inside, and I knew something was missing; but like always, I just said, "I'll figure it out. I'll take care of this." Well, as time went on, it got worse and worse. Everything in my life was falling apart and I was totally out of control. How was I going to fix this? How was I going to get back to "normal?" My anxiety was so high one day that I had a panic attack so severe that I couldn't go to work or even leave the house. It was 1:00 p.m. on a Monday, and I was turning up the bottle while the rest of the world went about as if I didn't exist. I knew at this point I needed help and needed it quickly.

After I answered that call on December 19, I was given the name and number to someone that might be able to help. I called him immediately hoping he would have all the answers to my problems and help fix me. After about 45 minutes, he painted two word pictures for me. The first was a life without Christ and the other was one with Christ. He asked me, "Which one do you want?" I said, "I want the second, but how do I get it? He said, "Just say this prayer with me and it's yours." Through my trembling voice and tear filled eyes, I had accepted Christ into my life.

Some amazing things started to happen almost immediately, and every day has gotten better and better. As I sit here today typing this short story, I can honestly say that I have more hope, faith and peace than I've had in over a decade. There are so many changes that I've made in my life that words on paper don't do it justice. When I wake up in the morning, I literally thank God for another day, and I'm working on my relationship with him constantly. I actually feel him sitting next to me as I type these words. Now I'm not "perfect" and

I know I have a lot to learn, but in my heart I believe that he is working through me, and I trust him!

There are so many details that I've left out of this story, but in the end, life's all about choices. I made a choice to accept Christ into my heart. With his help I'm going to do whatever I can to make sure that I don't go back to where I was before. And today, it's not cold and rainy but sunny and warm, and I'm more thankful for that than I could ever describe. I thank God for the people he's put in my life to help me realize this, and I hope that with his help, I can have the same positive impact on others as they've had on me. They know who they are, and I truly love them for that!

DAY 9

A Man's Talk

NOW THE WHOLE world had one language and a common speech.

As men moved eastward, they found a plain in Shinar and settled there. They said to each other, "Come, let's make bricks and bake them thoroughly." They used brick instead of stone, and tar for mortar. Then they said, "Come, let us build ourselves a city, with a tower that reaches to the heavens, so that we may make a name for ourselves and not be scattered over the face of the whole earth."

But the LORD came down to see the city and the tower that the men were building. The LORD said, "If as one people speaking the same language they have begun to do this, then nothing they plan to do will be impossible for them. Come, let us go down and confuse their language so they will not understand each other."

So the LORD scattered them from there over all the earth, and they stopped building the city. That is why it was called Babel—because there the LORD confused the language of the whole world. From there the LORD scattered them over the face of the whole earth.

(Gen. 11: 1-9)

Men form cultures that speak the same voice, each person shaping the other until they are of one mind. This talk occurs around football in the fall, basketball in the winter and baseball in the summer. We find it when listening to liberal or conservative talk radio. Even in a church, men gather and talk. And let's not forget about today's social media or gaming—spreading messages across groups and nations. Whether positive or negative, talk shapes the values and beliefs of those around us. It forms cultures. You determine much about a man's character by listening to his language and by listening to the words he values when speaking.

In what forums of talk do you participate? Are they angry, judgmental, or punitive? Do they promote the glory of God and love for mankind? Do they bring you and others closer to God? Would Jesus participate in them with you? Would He like your comments on Facebook, your language at the workout center, your conversations at church or around the coffee station? What would He think about your self-talk?

When men talk to each other to make a name for themselves and not God and the advancement of good, troubles begin. When men talk without a relationship with God, evil begins because nothing good comes from being apart from the Lord. Even talking to ourselves, (self-talk,) turns bad without prayer or without listening to God's words. This produces all kinds of anxieties, passivity, or poor behavior. It can crush the spirit.

Men of God do not boast.

Men of God realize that one reckless word or a few, like sparks, can set fire to a family or a nation.

Men of God do not curse other men.

Men of God do not gossip or talk about others without them present.

Men of God think and talk in five different perspectives, and in doing so, create cultures (families, teams, companies, and churches) around them.

- What is true
- What is noble
- What is right
- What is lovely
- What is admirable

When men talk about areas of improvement or change, they do so without anger and without blame and abuse, and without judgment, but with great power in the form of kindness, gentleness and patience. They speak about things with great strength—even passion—but without an attempt to harm or control their hearers. They protect the dignity of others, and they actually listen more than they talk. They speak the truth as they understand it and listen for the reply with humility. They admit when they are wrong.

The next time the talk begins, hang back and listen. Wait. Do not join in or respond until you understand the discussion and its context. If the talk isn't meeting one of the above perspectives, pray, then try to change its tone with your words and participation. If the person or those around you do not respond and continue their negative chatter, then get away from it.

Scatter (to another part of the world).

A MAN'S TALK
(your thoughts and actions)

What a man says and how he reacts to situations reflects years of habit, selfishness, perhaps bitterness, and a life apart from God or with Him. It can be altered through confession, prayer and a change of heart. As a man pursues knowing the Lord, His voice and His wisdom, he says "No" to the talk that he once allowed in from outside sources.

Only Jesus can make your heart new and your talk better.

How would those around you describe your character by what they hear you talk about?

_____

_____

_____

_____

_____

_____

If you are married, how does your talk affect the household—your wife and perhaps your children or grandchildren?

_____

_____

_____

_____

_____

_____

Do you focus on and complain about the world around you and the negatives you allow to flow into your ears and mind?

_____

_____

_____

_____

_____

What is your self-talk like? Is it quiet? Is it condemning? Is it full of anger toward others? Do you focus it on the past? Describe it.

_____

_____

_____

_____

_____

What you talk about can change the world. Your words reflect what you believe is true about God. They show the depth of your relationship with Him. One word from you can change a life forever—even your own.

DAY 10

A Man's Belief

HE TOOK HIM outside and said, "Look up at the heavens and count the stars–if indeed you can count them." Then he said to him, "So shall your offspring be."

Abram believed the LORD, and He credited it to him as righteousness.

Abram fell facedown, and God said to him, "As for me, this is my covenant with you: You will be the father of many nations. No longer will you be called Abram; your name will be Abraham, for I have made you a father of many nations. I will make you very fruitful; I will make nations of you, and kings will come from you. I will establish my covenant as an everlasting covenant between me and you and your descendants after you for the generations to come, to be your God and the God of your descendants after you. The whole land of Canaan, where you are now an alien, I will give as an everlasting possession to you and your descendants after you; and I will be their God."

Then God said to Abraham, "As for you, you must keep my covenant, you and your descendants after you for the generations to come.

(Gen. 15:5-6,17:3-9)

Think about how much your beliefs drive your life. What if someone told you that a purchase would sooth your soul and make life better? What if you believed that a few moments of pleasure would overcome the day's worries? What if you believed that a movie was worth seeing? What if it was clear to you that clothing "made the man"? What if you could only drink filtered water or eat salmon if it was from a specific ocean?

Which of your beliefs affect the car you choose or the house you purchase? What type of food do you think is best for you? What do you believe about being late to work or to a meeting? What do you believe about setting goals? How important is it to tell the truth, balance your checkbook, spend less than you earn, borrow to make a purchase, keep yourself physically fit, or pray to God?

You act on your beliefs 24/7, and what you REALLY believe drives your behavior. So, what do you believe about God and how does that affect your relationship with Him?

For example, do you REALLY believe that:

§ Jesus died for you and saved you from your sins because of your faith and not your works?
§ God walks with you, changes you, and directs your path in life?
§ The Lord will listen to you when you pray and answer your prayer?
§ In all things, God works for the good of those who love Him?
§ You are a child of God, dearly loved, and He has a place prepared for you in heaven?

God credits us as right-living men when we believe in Him—when we believe His promise; that He "gave His one and only Son, that whoever believes in Him shall not perish but have eternal life." The original Greek word (XXXXXX) for "believes" implies the kind of belief that a patriot has for his country— a living, sacrificial, trusting and faithful existence for a cause (that of Jesus Christ).

Having a living belief in God does not mean we enjoy a mistake-free life. It does mean that we accept responsibility when He shows us our folly and failure. It does mean we believe He will forgive us. It does mean He expects us to lean on His power to make changes and to find a new direction. It does mean that others will see a new man being changed and acting differently as a result of his faith and the power of God working in and through him.

Having a belief in God does not mean that we will live without experiencing tough times, disappointing results, or a crisis of faith. It does mean we look for Him to stand with us during moments of doubt and despair, or in times of great tragedy when we only have one finger left clinging to "the rock of our salvation."

As men of God, we believe what He says about everything. We know that our belief in Him saves us and for the rest of our life He will walk with us, change us, and move us in right directions. This is His promise, "to be with us until the end of the age." He WILL listen to us when we talk to Him. He WILL give us wisdom and work in our favor in all kinds of circumstances. He WILL be with us.

Men, believe in Him and hold onto your faith. Live it out each day and think of this. Through you, many generations may find His everlasting covenant of peace. This only takes one man. You.

~ ~ ~

A MAN'S BELIEF
(your thoughts and actions)

What did Abraham believe about God?

That He was all kowing & He would deliver

What do you believe about God?

I believe God is the all good an
kowing perfect leving eternal
being that loves us and is
the base and foundation for
all that is good.

How do your beliefs about God drive your behaviors during the day? Do
you think He is with you? Do you think He cares about you? Do you
think He will direct you? Describe what your faith looks like to yourself
and to those around you.

My belief in God leads to my
hope, joy, and repentance.
I know that I serve a mighty king

Is what you believe true? What is it based on?

yes. Bible speaks only truth

A MAN'S DISCOVERY

Today, read the Bible on your own, for your own reasons, and ask God to reveal Himself to you. Ask him to reveal something you need to know. Pursue Him in this way. Pursue Him in prayer. As you learn, pursue Him in obedience.

Here's what the Bible says is true about itself. "All Scripture is God-breathed and is useful for teaching, rebuking, correcting and training in righteousness, so that the man of God may be thoroughly equipped for every good work." (2 Tim. 3: 16-18)

We live in a broken and decaying world. That's why people hurt other people. This began centuries ago and we see it in our talk, decisions and actions. They are signposts in our lives screaming out to God and the world what we believe.

There are things that are true, whether we think or feel they are true or not. Here's one. Look at the cross. Jesus loves you.

What you believe and where you put your trust makes a difference. Do you know God?

DAY 11

A Man's Desperate Decisions

NOW THERE WAS a famine in the land, and Abram went down to Egypt to live there for a while because the famine was severe. As he was about to enter Egypt, he said to his wife Sarai, "I know what a beautiful woman you are. When the Egyptians see you, they will say, 'This is his wife.' Then they will kill me but will let you live. Say you are my sister, so that I will be treated well for your sake and my life will be spared because of you."

When Abram came to Egypt, the Egyptians saw that she was a very beautiful woman. And when Pharaoh's officials saw her, they praised her to Pharaoh, and she was taken into his palace. He treated Abram well for her sake, and Abram acquired sheep and cattle, male and female donkeys, menservants and maidservants, and camels.

But the LORD inflicted serious diseases on Pharaoh and his household because of Abram's wife Sarai. So Pharaoh summoned Abram. "What have you done to me?" he said. "Why didn't you tell me she was your wife? Why did you say, 'She is my sister,' so that I took her to be my wife? Now then, here is your wife. Take her and go!" Then Pharaoh gave orders about Abram to his men, and they sent him on his way, with his wife and everything he had.

(Gen. 12:10-20)

~ ~ ~

Look at your job, your family and your past choices. How did you act when times were tough or you were stressed? What parts of yourself did you compromise to survive? Were you honest? Did you speak the truth? Could those close to you trust you? Did you lash out in anger? Did you fall apart, display negative emotions or criticize without thinking?

It's difficult to maintain my integrity during times of turbulence and chaos. There are things I know in my heart are true, but in practice I forget who I am in Christ when times get hard.

I have never been in danger of losing my life because of my faith in Him or because of my nationality. Others have, but I have not. Others have been martyred. I have not. Others have withstood an ultimate test upon their resolve. I have not, and I do not know how I would respond.

I would like to say that I'm tough enough to spit in the face of a threat. In reality I know that I have, more times than I want to remember, compromised what I believe just to have fun or respect or a position. I wanted to save something I desired more than to remain a good soldier, a friend of Christ, or a protector of those around me.

I have also stood my ground at the right time and the wrong time. I made the decision. I stopped the actions or the words of those in front of me for the protection of others or for taking a stand against unrighteous behavior. There were times that God compelled me. There were times I simply acted out of a judgmental attitude and without the direction of Christ. I once walked away from $5000 per month because my client would not pay my friend what he was due in commission. On the other hand, I once asked someone to stop their cursing to make a point, and I lost my continued ability to be an influence in the lives of several other people.

What about you?

Doing the right thing when stressed or worried occurs by leaning on the wisdom and might and peacefulness of the Lord. Some of us are just in the beginning of that wisdom and we still follow the crowd or behave with old habits. Even those further down the journey with Christ still make mistakes when thinking of the personal cost of action or inaction.

This I know. My own actions and behavior can, as time passes, change into those of Christ Jesus. I can be changed by His power into a new man who makes better decisions and acts in a right manner during desperate or stress-filled times. I can turn and apologize. I can make amends. I can keep my mouth in check. I can remain calm, patient, and act with kindness. I cannot do these things alone or in my own effort, but I can do these things with the power of Christ Jesus. Even if I deny Him at the point of trial, I can find His forgiveness as a man named Peter did years ago.

Here are some things for men to remember from saints of long ago...

- § "Blessed is the man who perseveres under trial, because when he has stood the test, he will receive the crown of life that God has promised to those who love him." (James 1:12)
- § "We boast about your perseverance and faith in all the persecutions and trials you are enduring." (2 Thess. 1:4)
- § "Out of the most severe trial, their overflowing joy and their extreme poverty welled up in rich generosity." (2 Cor. 8:2)
- § "... you may have had to suffer grief in all kinds of trials. These have come so that your faith—of greater worth than gold, which perishes even though refined by fire—may

be proved genuine and may result in praise, glory and honor when Jesus Christ is revealed." (1 Peter 1:6-7)

§ "And I tell you that you are Peter, and on this rock I will build my church, and the gates of Hades will not overcome it." (Matt. 16:18)

Remember, Jesus is the rock and you are a rock!

~ ~ ~

A MAN'S DESPERATE DECISIONS
(your thoughts and actions)

Abraham, a man of great faith in God, prostituted his wife and put her in harms way because he was afraid that he would die. What are 3-5 of the worst decisions you have made?

_____

_____

_____

_____

_____

_____

How did prayer to God play a part in your previous decisions? Did you wait before you acted and look for His leading? Did you obey what you knew was true in your heart?

_____

_____

_____

_____

_____

_____

Read Proverbs 3:5-6. What does this say about a man's decisions?

_____

_____

_____

_____

_____

What does God put into our hearts as a seal of ownership and righteous-ness in Christ? (2 Cor. 1:22; Eph. 1:13-14)

His spirit , Holy spirit

What do these words say about the Spirit of God, which He places in those who give their lives to Christ? (Rom. 8:12-14)

That we have the ability to be free from Sin (Slavery) and be adopted as Gods own children.

Later in life, after his failure with Sarah, Abraham was told by God to sacrifice his only son, and he raised his sword to do so. God stopped him and said, "I swear by myself that because you have done this and have not withheld your son, your only son, I will surely bless you and make your descendants as numerous as the stars in the sky and as the sand on the seashore. Your descendants will take possession of the cities of their enemies, and through your offspring all nations on earth will be blessed, because you have obeyed me."

Obey God in times of desperation. His Spirit will lead you.

A Man's Signposts

ABRAHAM WAS NOW old and well advanced in years, and the LORD had blessed him in every way. He said to the chief servant in his household, the one in charge of all that he had, "Put your hand under my thigh. I want you to swear by the LORD, the God of heaven and the God of earth, that you will not get a wife for my son from the daughters of the Canaanites, among whom I am living, but will go to my country and my own relatives and get a wife for my son Isaac."

After miles of travel, Abraham's servant had the camels kneel down near the well outside the town; it was toward evening, the time the women go out to draw water. Then he prayed, "O LORD, God of my master Abraham, give me success today, and show kindness to my master Abraham. See, I am standing beside this spring, and the daughters of the townspeople are coming out to draw water. May it be that when I say to a girl, 'Please let down your jar that I may have a drink,' and she says, 'Drink, and I'll water your camels too'-let her be the one you have chosen for your servant Isaac. By this I will know that you have shown kindness to my master."

Before he had finished praying, Rebekah came out with her jar on her shoulder. She was the daughter of Bethuel son of Milcah, who was the wife of Abraham's brother Nahor. The girl was very beautiful, a virgin; no man had ever lain with her. She went down to the spring, filled her jar and came up again. The servant hurried to meet her and said, "Please give me a little water from your jar." "Drink, my lord," she said, and quickly lowered the jar to her hands and gave him a drink.

After she had given him a drink, she said, "I'll draw water for your camels too, until they have finished drinking." So she quickly emptied her jar into the trough, ran back to the well to draw more water, and drew enough for all his camels. Without saying a word, the man watched her closely to learn whether or not the LORD had made his journey successful. Then he asked, "Whose daughter are you? Please tell me, is there room in your father's house for us to spend the night?" She answered him, "I am the daughter of Bethuel, the son that Milcah bore to Nahor." And she added, "We have plenty of straw and fodder, as well as room for you to spend the night."

Then the man bowed down and worshiped the LORD, saying, "Praise be to the LORD, the God of my master Abraham, who has not abandoned his kindness and faithfulness to my master. As for me, the LORD has led me on the journey to the house of my master's relatives."

(Gen. 24:1-4,11-23, 26-27)

What's it like to start out on a new journey? What's it like to do this without God? I know. Do you?

I know what it's like to jump into things and start swinging. I know what it's like to make a decision and get on with it. I also know what it's like to be indecisive and to just sit on my backside. I know what it's like to react without thinking, with anger, or without any acknowledgment that God exists at all. I know. I really know. Do you?

What about those times when you know God wants you to do something—to lead a project or to serve others in a particular way? First of all, do you know what it's like to be led by God? Then, do you know what it feels like to do things without Him? Do you know what it's like to be uncertain about your next step or how you will accomplish an important objective, or to be paralyzed by indecision? Do you know what it's like to need Him to really need His presence for difficult decisions and complex situations? Perhaps you need to have a "crucial conversation" with your bride, or your son, a boss, or a co-worker. Before you act, do you go to Him for advice? Do you expect Him to lead you, to guide you, to direct your path? Do you?

How do you start each day—in prayer, with a to-do list or with talk radio in the car? Do you just swing your legs out of bed, stumble to the bathroom and start the morning routine?

Many of us move into the day without a discussion with our Father. We believe in Him, but it's as if He made the world, gave it a big spin, and then remained unattached looking at it with curiosity to see what we shall do. Or, even worse, slaps us around when we are bad.

And yet, it's simple, like a perfect Father's intense love toward his newborn child. He pays attention to every change in your condition.

He wants you to know His presence. He wants to protect you, to lead you, and to observe your every movement. He wants to help you in this broken world. He wants you to be with Him. He wants you to trust Him no matter the circumstances. He wants to discipline you, to test you and discipline you and refine you. Through danger, sickness, great toil, hunger, persecution, pain, and what the decaying world brings, He wants to lead you. Believe this. He is good. He will be there. Will you?

Years ago, my bride Sheila experienced a time in which her heart was exposed to a spirit of fear. This occurred during the painful uncertainty of many financial difficulties God used to shape our desire for Him. While I was absent looking for myself, for God and income, and Sheila was taking care of our children, she felt great loneliness and separation clutch her heart. As she was driving home, doubt and fear began to crush her. She found herself crying out in her mind, "God, are you there? Are you real? Please, help me! Show me you're with me!" Immediately she raised her eyes and there in front of her was the most beautiful rainbow arching across the sky—the first she had seen since her childhood, and its colors fell across the horizon as if to say, "See, my child, I am with you." Today, every time she relives that moment, tears begin to trickle down her face as she remembers.

I can also tell you of many times when I felt fearful or discouraged and God answered when I called out to Him. As I look back, I see his responses sometimes stretched out over several months and years. I can also confess, even in recent times, forgetting to ask, forgetting to talk with Him, forgetting His power and His love. Yet today, I am better at remembering the Lord. I am better at being His child. I am better and closer in an everyday relationship with Jesus.

Men who are led by the Spirit of God are sons of God. God does not give them a spirit of timidity, but a spirit of power, of love and of self-discipline.

He allows you to choose living with Him or without Him. At times He pursues you, and at times He waits for you to return.

Ask for a sign. Ask!

He will not abandon His kindness and faithfulness to you.

He will lead you on your journey.

A MAN'S SIGNPOSTS
(your thoughts and actions)

How old are you? No matter the age, the signposts have come and gone. What do you remember as monument building moments in your life—the times that have helped you learn the most?

_____

_____

_____

_____

_____

What have you learned from the struggle of challenging times? Read Romans 8:28. How did God work in those times? What was he trying to teach you?

_____

_____

_____

_____

_____

Our responses to these times give us the ability to strengthen our faith, rebel, or retreat into the things that help us forget. How have you responded?

_____

_____

_____

_____

What is your relationship with Jesus? Describe it. How is that relationship personal and not distant?

_____

_____

_____

_____

_____

_____

Men who are led by the Spirit of God are sons of God. The apostle Paul reminds us in his message to Timothy that, "God did not give us a spirit of timidity, but a spirit of power, of love and of self-discipline." (2 Tim. 1:7)

I want you to know that God allows you to choose an existence without Him or with Him. However, He does look for you, His prodigal son. At times, He even pursues you. At other times, He waits for your return. Read the signs. They all point back to Him.

"Then, leaving her water jar, the woman went back to the town and said to the people, "Come, see a man who told me everything I ever did. Could this be the Christ?" They came out of the town and made their way toward him."

John 4:28-30

A Man Moved by God

Could This Be the Christ?

SEVERAL YEARS AGO, a 14 year-old young man stepped off of a school bus one hot day in Texas. Summer was on its way. As he was walking home, he was invited over to a friend's house for some fun with a few guys from the neighborhood. He walked with them to an older guy's house and gathered with them in the garage. When this naive 14 year-old young man entered the garage he would later discover that what happened that day would change his life forever. He got high for the first time.

The weeks passed by and I started going to the garage more often, but before long these trips got old and lost their excitement. A year after my new high, I found myself at another friend's house staying the night. In the early morning, his sister helped me experience something new that was nothing like the garage stuff. It was so much more intense and made me feel strong and bullet proof like I was ten feet tall!!!!!!!! This was IT. This is what I was really looking for—I used 'meth' for the first time.

The year that I turned 17, I took Ecstasy as well and was left freezing in the emergency room driveway of a hospital. I was treated for a drug overdose. I was also involved with a drug enforcement sting operation that could have placed me in jail until age 34. For some 'reason,' outside of me, I stood at the back of a police car and realized for the first time I was NOT in control, and I asked GOD for help, and He listened.

I continued a self-destructive and drug abusing lifestyle. I even found myself facing jail time again for violent assault on another young man in an apartment complex. However, for some 'reason' he could not remember the specifics of the assault. The substance in his system kept him from remembering exactly what happened. I was saved again.

But then something amazing happened. I walked into an apartment one day and realized the only way I could continue in life and experience any amount of joy was to understand that my life was not my own and that I had been created for something more. I realized that Christ was interested in my entire life and He could still make use of even the darkest parts of it.

I am a little older now and I have a wife who loves me, not for what I was, but for who Christ has made me. I also have a little girl whom both of us agree we have been given by Jesus. Each day, we give her back to Him. I have also learned, that each day, the most fulfilling thing I can do is to help those around me see that even their garage moments can be used to glorify Him and to help someone else.

I started to find myself approached by people who help others work through spiritual challenges. They call themselves Christians. I remember a specific day and moment that occurred after I had started to give my daily temptations over to Christ. I was warring with temptation and found myself wanting to give into what I at one time called "needs." Then, there was a knock at my apartment door from a guy who ran a faith-based consulting program for people with drug issues, and he asked me to come speak to his group of about 50 or so. ME!!!!!! What did I know? Why in the world would he ask me? That's when I realized my darkness could be used to bring light to others. Month after month, God continued to put these types of opportunities into my path.

While participating in the addiction program, I realized I had a place among God's people. So, I started surrounding myself with more and more of them. This made the warfare easier. I continued on my spiritual journey and began a college and career class for college-aged people at the same church that hosted the addiction program.

The discussions with the students in the class helped me realize that everyone is at war with something. I hosted these college-aged students in Bible studies, and we met with the hope that we could all find answers to really hard stuff. Some really good things happened there because of God's intervention.

I moved to Tennessee to attend a seminary where I received an associate's degree in religion. I found out that religion without Jesus can scare people away from Him. I also learned that God does not require action to earn what Jesus did for us. He requires faith. I also met the love of my life and we began dating. I thought this was a miracle because I would find myself saying WHAT!?—and thinking there was no way that she would ever want to be with me. I would tell myself, "You're just some druggie!" But then God would remind me that he had changed me into a new man—*His man!*

Brooke and I dated and became crazy in love, but I soon learned that when you become a Christian there are still trials. Brooke's father passed away unexpectedly. As I write this, I am realizing for the first time that this was when I witnessed faith during tragedy. God prepared us then for the passing of my mother three years later.

The temptations of a young druggie linger, but God restrains them. Each time they challenged me, I ended up faced with an opportunity to share my story with someone. Weird huh? It's as if God says, "Hey, as a matter of fact why don't you tell these people what I did about that for you."

In 2011, I married Brooke Danielle Cole. This moment helped me realize that God does not hold grudges (a thought that ironically at the time I wrestled with). If He had, He would not have given me such a perfect lady. ▯

In November of 2014, we saw God deliver Violet Adele Bledsoe into the world. With her arrival, we learned to submit all we possessed to God. When Brooke was expecting, we worried about a miscarriage. We got through the first three months and then we hoped through the next three. The next three came and we "hoped" for a smooth delivery. and then we found ourselves afraid of things like Sudden Infant Death Syndrome and crib suffocation. But God was in control of all things, and we realized WE HAD STEPPED INTO A NEW LEVEL OF CHALLENGES all of which would be handled by GOD.

Today, this young man is still alive and some might call him "successful." He even has a little bit of godly influence on others, and an opportunity to give more credit to his Jesus Christ, his rescuer. Without Him, he would be a young man that walked into a garage one day and never returned to life. And his story continues ...

DAY 13

Men Stop the Cycle!

SO ISAAC STAYED in Gerar. When the men of that place asked him about his wife, he said, "She is my sister," because he was afraid to say, "She is my wife." He thought, "The men of this place might kill me on account of Rebekah, because she is beautiful." When Isaac had been there a long time, Abimelech king of the Philistines looked down from a window and saw Isaac caressing his wife Rebekah.

So Abimelech summoned Isaac and said, "She is really your wife! Why did you say, 'She is my sister'?"

Isaac answered him, "Because I thought I might lose my life on account of her." Then Abimelech said, "What is this you have done to us? One of the men might well have slept with your wife, and you would have brought guilt upon us."

So Abimelech gave orders to all the people: "Anyone who molests this man or his wife shall surely be put to death."

(Just as his father, Abraham, Isaac put his wife in jeopardy to protect his own life.)

(Gen. 26:6-11)

Years ago, our English Shepherd, Muffie, used to meet us when we returned home by running up into the woods barking at the approach of our car. It seemed as though she did this to make sure nothing would harm us as we arrived. That wonderful dog trained our next dog to do the same thing, and the cycle continued for years.

Mountain lions teach their cubs how to stalk their prey. Birds teach their young to fly. Foxes teach their kits how to hunt at night. Like father, like son, farmers pass on their skills to their sons. From one man to the next, the skills AND the sins of the father are passed from one generation to the next.

Did you know your Father? Did you catch his sins? Did he pass on the same bad behaviors as his father, grandfather or great grandfather? Today, are you a living, duplicating machine in some of the ways you react and behave?

Do you sin in the same way as your forefathers? Do you know if they were swindlers, alcoholics, or adulterers? Did they lie, eat excessively, or avoid working? Did their emotions spill out in angry words, or did their judgment strike out in criticism or their fists hit others with power?

The Bible says, "He committed all the sins his father had done before him; his heart was not fully devoted to the LORD his God... He did evil in the eyes of the LORD, walking in the ways of his father and in his sin, which he had caused Israel to commit...You shall not bow down to them or worship them; for I, the LORD your God, am a jealous God, punishing the children for the sin of the fathers to the third and fourth generation of those who hate me... or visiting the iniquity of the fathers on the children to the third and fourth generation of those who hate me ... but showing love to a thousand generations of those who love me and keep my commandments (1 Kings 15:3, 26; ; Ex. 20: 5-6).

Science says, "The Biblical prediction turns out to be more complex than anyone thought: the lifestyle sins of fathers can be visited on their children and are passed on in ways we are only beginning to understand. (http://tinyurl.com/q86u7hm ... "Stress levels and smoking: Why your dad's bad habits may have wrecked your genes"). By the way, as the Bible also says, research is also showing you CAN change your tendencies and behaviors.

~ ~ ~

No matter what science says, you CAN stop your tendencies and create new habits with the power of God. With Him, you CAN stop the things you do not want to do.

God will show love to a thousand generations for those who love Him and keep His commands.

RESCUED!...

The apostle Paul once said, "For in my inner being I delight in God's law; but I see another law at work in the members of my body, waging war against the law of my mind and making me a prisoner of the law of sin at work within my members. What a wretched man I am! Who will rescue me from this body of death? Thanks be to God–through Jesus Christ our Lord! (Rom. 7:22-25).

LIFE AND PEACE...

"The mind of sinful man is death, but the mind controlled by the Spirit is life and peace; the sinful mind is hostile to God. It does not submit to God's law, nor can it do so. Those controlled by the sinful nature cannot please God. You, however, are controlled not by the sinful nature but by the Spirit, if the Spirit of God lives in you" (Rom. 8:6-9).

RIGHTEOUSNESS AND PEACE...

"Our fathers disciplined us for a little while as they thought best; but God disciplines us for our good, that we may share in his holiness. No discipline seems pleasant at the time, but painful. Later on, however, it produces a harvest of righteousness and peace for those who have been trained by it" (Heb. 12:10-12).

DISCIPLINED BY GOD...

Go through the pain of change—the crucible of God's spirit. It's worth it. You can endure it with Him. Keep praying. Keep getting up. Keep reading and listening to God's words. Keep smiling. Keep striving. Keep on keeping on. Bring love to the next generation! FREEDOM!

And while you are growing, remember, "There is no condemnation in Christ Jesus—only grace and forgiveness!"

MEN STOP THE CYCLE
(your thoughts and actions)

What behaviors, habits, or addictions do you want to stop in your generation? What do you want God to stop with you? Tell Him right now.

_____

_____

_____

_____

_____

Sometimes men live out life with fear, a lack of forgiveness, and a hidden vow deep within them as a result of not wanting to be what they saw expressed in their families as a child. Sadly, when they make this vow out of their own power, they sometimes move in that direction anyway. Ask God to change you and take the fear away and allow you to behave by His power in you and not by yours.

_____

_____

_____

_____

_____

Pray that generational sin will be stamped out by the renewal of Spirit-led men beginning with you and then with the generations to come.

In prayer, admit you are powerless without God and that you can do all things in Christ who strengthens you.

This is a time of prayer and reflection and perhaps victory as you realize God's handiwork in redeeming your life, and the peace and joy you now experience at times that comes from Him.

It can also be a serious time of great turmoil for others. I encourage you. Keep on keeping on with the KING of kings. He will be your rock—forever! Peace.

The One Man Who Rescues

NOW ISRAEL LOVED Joseph more than any of his other sons, because he had been born to him in his old age; and he made a richly ornamented robe for him. When his brothers saw that their father loved him more than any of them, they hated him and could not speak a kind word to him.

Joseph had a dream, and when he told it to his brothers, they hated him all the more. He said to them, "Listen to this dream I had: We were binding sheaves of grain out in the field when suddenly my sheaf rose and stood upright, while your sheaves gathered around mine and bowed down to it." His brothers said to him, "Do you intend to reign over us? Will you actually rule us?" And they hated him all the more because of his dream and what he had said.

So Joseph went after his brothers and found them near Dothan. But they saw him in the distance, and before he reached them, they plotted to kill him. "Here comes that dreamer!" they said to each other. "Come now, let's kill him and throw him into one of these cisterns and say that a ferocious animal devoured him. Then we'll see what comes of his dreams."

When Reuben (Joseph's older brother) heard this, he tried to rescue him from their hands. "Let's not take his life," he said. "Don't shed any blood. Throw him into this cistern here in the desert, but don't lay a hand on him." Reuben said this to rescue him from them and take him back to his father.

(Gen. 37:3-8,17-22)

When men look around them, they see what appears to be a lack of fairness in the world; poor men and rich men; hunger and famine; new homes and cardboard dwellings. Steeped in prejudice or respected with kindness, children walk around barefoot in the dirt within large families or as orphans, tall and small, black and white.

In church, another picture appears where different men sit in different pews. Some talk in this corner, others talk in that corner. One group to the east, the other to the west. Some like color and others like black and white. Some raise their hands and clap, while others sit in solemn stillness. Some sit in the back pews, some in the front ones; some arrive early, some late.

A family raises children with 12 boys. Some are good at sports, while others work with their hands or play the piano. Some like the outdoors, but others like to draw in their rooms. Some make people laugh, and some are easily depressed or sad. Then there's the one, the special one, the gifted one, and all the others must fade away for this one, and like Joseph, his brothers hate him because he's favored by his father.

It's better for men to praise God in whatever state they find themselves, whether in plenty or in want. Life isn't fair, but God is good.

In the shelters provided for people who need a place to sleep and food to eat, I've seen men steal from one another out of the personal possessions piled beside a cot. I've seen men scared for their children and for their family. In that same setting, I've seen the beauty of a man's heart as one gave to another out of poverty.

I've seen a man who lived in humble surroundings praise another who lived a rich life. I've seen a man work in the treetops, in danger and needing money for food, while another worked in an office skyscraper and bought coffee at Starbucks; and then on one special day, I saw them meet and laugh like brothers. I've seen men smile no matter their condition. I've seen one man stand and rescue another.

It's not as easy to see these things while listening to the soft sound of a heating and air system keeping the air at 72 degrees. It's easier to see these things in Louisiana after a hurricane or in Alabama around tornado-destroyed homes, and it's easier to talk about rescuing someone when you've needed saving yourself. When you've gone through tough times, you begin to overlook the surface differences you see in the people around you.

We are all rich in Christ—the yellow, the blue, the hungry, the full, the singer and the laborer.

We are all children of God.

We are all grateful.

We are all living and dying.

We are all gifted.

We are all loved by God.

I have not learned the secret of being content in any and every situation, whether well fed or hungry, whether living in plenty or in want. I have not learned to keep my head in all situations, to endure hardship, to do the work God gives me as a ministry without complaint. But, I am growing and changing into a better man.

Be the one man who rescues.

Be the one man who does the peacemaking.

Be the one man who remembers Jesus.

Work hard against the grain, as the Spirit leads you, and just keep making a difference. You can do everything through Him who gives you strength.

THE ONE MAN WHO RESCUES
(your thoughts and actions)

Who can you help today? Who can you encourage?

_____

_____

_____

_____

_____

_____

Who can you mentor?

_____

_____

_____

_____

_____

_____

Where can you give some time or money to someone who needs it?

_____

_____

_____

_____

_____

_____

Who can you comfort?

_____

_____

_____

_____

_____

_____

You're a man. This is a great adventure. People are in battles all around you. Protect them. Fight for them. Help them and sleep well.

Men Who Struggle with God

SO JACOB WAS left alone, and a man wrestled with him till day-break. When the man saw that he could not overpower him, he touched the socket of Jacob's hip so that his hip was wrenched as he wrestled with the man.

Then the man said, "Let me go, for it is daybreak."

But Jacob replied, "I will not let you go unless you bless me."

The man asked him, "What is your name?"

"Jacob," he answered.

Then the man said, "Your name will no longer be Jacob, but Israel, because you have struggled with God and with men and have overcome."

Jacob said, "Please tell me your name."

But he replied, "Why do you ask my name?"

Then he blessed him there.

So Jacob called the place Peniel, saying, "It is because I saw God face to face, and yet my life was spared."

(Gen. 32:24-30)

Sometimes life smashes you in the face with the anxiety of problems and uncertainty. Whether family, finances, job, transportation, or home, various parts of life break into unresolved pieces, and God doesn't seem to bless anything. Fear reaches inside you and stirs your heart with doubt. Out of our loneliness we strive and flounder. When we realize we cannot control or change it, we fight without rules, we either run, or we look to God.

There was a time in my life when I couldn't see a way out. My guilt was mixed in confusion and darkness and I sought answers in places that made things worse. I slid through the day not really facing any of the problems and I made decisions based on unwise counsel. As I continued down this rabbit hole, what was a wonderland adventure turned into a nightmare of ever-compressing dimensions without answers for my escape.

I remember having two choices: (1) Stop trying, leave my family and go to Florida, or (2) Give everything up to God and struggle with Him in my situation. I was inexperienced with the latter.

He led me to the second choice and I gave up the fight. I'd like to say that my "road less traveled" was the easy one—the one that made things better immediately—the one that eased my way. It did not. The way was grievous and painful. Things in me were dislocated, torn apart, and put back together. But afterwards, God's training and discipline brought more peace and right living to me and my family.

If you bring the Lord into your life, He will participate in all your struggles for the rest of your life. You may notice a minor skirmish over what the Spirit of God says to your conscience regarding how you just treated your wife or the cashier at the grocery store. There may be several times when God dislocates everything in you and around you just to help you grow as a man. Actually, life with Him is a lifetime struggle of joyous new beginnings that all of us can find in our relationship with Jesus who spares us and changes us.

I write to you, young men, because you have overcome the evil one. (1 John 2:13)

Remember His words...

"I will make you a wall to this people,

a fortified wall of bronze;

they will fight against you

but will not overcome you,

for I am with you

to rescue and save you," declares the LORD. (Jer. 15:20)

Do not be overcome by evil, but overcome evil with good. (Rom 12:21)

He who overcomes will inherit all this, and I will be his God and he will be my son. (Rev. 21:1-7)

- - -

MEN WHO STRUGGLE WITH GOD
(your thoughts and actions)

Are you honest with God? Do you speak to Him about how you feel and think and about what confuses you? Are you REALLY honest with God? If yes, write yes, if no, write down what area of your life you presently hide from Him as if He cannot see it.

_____

_____

_____

_____

_____

Read the words from this verse in the Bible. (1 Chr. 29:17) David is talking about the people's generous giving to the building of the temple. What does he say God tests and is pleased with?

_____

_____

_____

_____

_____

Are you angry with God? Bad things happen in this broken world, and when we cannot make sense of them we sometimes blame God by saying, "He could have stopped it." Is there something you need to wrestle with Him about? If so, write it down and with an open heart discuss it with Him with all your emotions and thoughts that surround it.

_____

_____

_____

_____

_____

When we read the stories in the Bible, we find men there who are not perfect and who try to live apart from God. Yet, those who are blessed bring their fractured souls to Him with honest intent. Start the day and ask God to bless you and your family, and be specific with the areas of your life in which you wish His entrance and transforming power.

_____

_____

_____

_____

_____

Fight to bring Him deeper into your life and the lives of others. Labor "with all His energy, which so powerfully works in you (Col. 1:29)." He saves us all. He gives you strength.

Men Can Be Trusted

FROM THE TIME he put him in charge of his household and of all that he owned, the LORD blessed the household of the Egyptian because of Joseph. The blessing of the LORD was on everything Potiphar had, both in the house and in the field.

So he left in Joseph's care everything he had; with Joseph in charge, he did not concern himself with anything except the food he ate.

Now Joseph was well built and handsome, and after a while his master's wife took notice of Joseph and said, "Come to bed with me!"

But he refused. "With me in charge," he told her, "my master does not concern himself with anything in the house; everything he owns he has entrusted to my care. No one is greater in this house than I am. My master has withheld nothing from me except you, because you are his wife. How then could I do such a wicked thing and sin against God?" And though she spoke to Joseph day after day, he refused to go to bed with her or even be with her.

One day he went into the house to attend to his duties, and none of the household servants was inside. She caught him by his cloak and said, "Come to bed with me!" But he left his cloak in her hand and ran out of the house.

When his master heard the story that his wife told him, saying, "This is how your slave treated me," he burned with anger. Joseph's master took him and put him in prison, the place where the king's prisoners were confined. But while Joseph was there in the prison, the LORD was with him; he showed him kindness and granted him favor in the eyes of the prison warden.

(The entire is story is here, in Gen. 39:5-21)

Let's say that we awake today and all is like in the beginning—no pain, no worries, no danger. God blesses what you touch and everything is perfect—perfect world, perfect bride, perfect relationship with the God of the uerse. All you see is entrusted into your care and you have permission to do all things, except for one thing: one piece of fruit from one tree. Or, one girl, one time, one forbidden moment. What would you do?

When the Lord of lords looks at today's newspaper, or watches the workplace and the homes of men, or attends a sporting event, what does He see? What does He hear when He listens to the nation's radio? What does He experience when He views the movies we love? What does He see over our shoulder when we turn on our computers, our iPads, or our smart phones?

All of us see men, entrusted with a sphere of influence and property, make decisions in their own best interest. They do this without consideration of others or with good stewardship as defined by God. Men waste what they have, tear down instead of build, hoard instead of share, grab for power, and do what's wrong in dark places. Or, they just sit by and watch and smother their talents, while others take on the challenges and responsibilities necessary for working out the trust they have been given.

What does it mean for someone to trust you, to put their confidence in you, to give you a position of duty and obligation? What does purity look like—to be virtuous, to be innocent, to act with honor?

Sometimes it means turn a television off. Sometimes it means run from or avoid compromising situations. Sometimes it means fight what is in front of you and sometimes it means run from it. It most often means sacrificing yourself or getting rid of something that draws you into addiction.

You have been given a position of respect and trust at great cost—the suffering, death, and resurrection of Jesus Christ. As a result of this saving act, and belief in Him, you have been given the following titles: saints, children of God, friends of Jesus, sons of God.

Now, as men of God, you realize your high position of exceptional value as displayed on a cross when you were unworthy. Accepting this position, obtained by the painful sacrifice of Jesus, you desire to grow, and in doing so, you begin to:

§ Reject passivity
§ Accept responsibility
§ Lead courageously
§ Act with honor

… all for things that last, and to rebuild a better world today and for future generations.

You do this because you walk with Jesus and like-minded men, depend on the Spirit of God, and pray for the day and its challenges and decisions. You fight the battles against good and evil as a superhero representing Jesus and the good news. Your family sees this, your co-workers see this, and your buddies see this.

MEN CAN BE TRUSTED
(your thoughts and actions)

Who are the most trustworthy men you know around you—men who meet their commitments and responsibilities?

_____

_____

_____

_____

_____

_____

What impact do these men have on you and the people around them?

_____

_____

_____

_____

_____

_____

What happens when a person does not act in a trustworthy manner? What's the effect?

_____

_____

_____

_____

_____

_____

Take a look at your finances, other assets, and relationships. Which of these needs the most attention at this time? Pray about this and then write down what actions you will do to honor your management in this area.

_____

_____

_____

_____

_____

How does pornography impact your integrity?

_____

_____

_____

_____

_____

You are a man of God, and it's a new day. Now, go and do what is right in His power. Find victory in one prayerful decision and action at a time, and find the ultimate victory already won by the King of kings. Get up, be watchful, and lead those around you. This may cost you in the short term, but it will work itself out for eternity. May God be with you and give you his favor and kindness.

"In all your ways acknowledge Him, and He will direct your paths."

Proverbs 3:6 (ASV)

A Man Moved by God

Acknowledge Him in All My Ways

I WAS RAISED in a good home. While my parents were godly examples, they didn't talk to me very much about their faith. Instead, most of my spiritual teaching came from the church we attended which, unfortunately, focused on doctrinal correctness and external measures of spiritual growth (e.g., church attendance and good works). I grew up not understanding what it means to have a relationship with God. Nevertheless, as I grew, I moved naturally into a leadership position in the same church, although I rarely prayed (except as required to do so in public) and only studied God's word in preparation to teach a class.

I started a business and God granted me success, although I didn't acknowledge His hand in my success. On one occasion, a Christian brother remarked how God had blessed me, and I recall thinking, "Well, maybe, but I am successful due to my hard work." I had allowed pride to take control of my life. I loved wearing the identity of a "successful" businessman, and I reveled in the accolades of men. I also became focused on money, and I obsessed about material possessions. I owned land, boats, and a lake condo. I took expensive vacations. Almost all of my extra time was spent in managing my possessions and planning fun experiences. Life was good ... or so I thought.

Ultimately, I sold my business and had enough cash to retire at the age of 53 if I had lived a frugal lifestyle. But pride and materialism would not allow me to do so. I followed my pride into two other businesses—one as a partner in real estate development and the other as an investor in a medical services company. I thought that diversifying my investments would hedge against losses. I was wrong—It doubled my losses.

The bottom fell out. My real estate partner and I had leveraged our investment to borrow over three million dollars to purchase commercial and residential properties. Before the "great recession" we could have sold it all for almost twice as much as we owed. However, during the spring of 2008, it became obvious that the property was not worth what we owed on it. Even if it was, no one was buying land at appraised value. During the same month, I attended a board meeting for the medical services company where the majority owner announced that he was shutting down the company. In an instant, I lost much of my cash and owed the bank much more than was left.

I was devastated. My identity as a successful businessman was ruined. I was a complete failure. My financial security was also gone. I was fifty-five years old and facing bankruptcy. Starting over scared me to death, and I had nowhere to turn. I remember crying out to God for help.

I had to quickly sell almost everything to reduce my payments and recover what little cash I could. I sold my lake condo at a great loss, my boat (that I loved), my guitar, and anything else of value. I had to sell the house that my son and his wife were living in at college and they had to move. Ultimately, I sold my personal house at a loss and moved out of town to follow a business opportunity (and, I think in retrospect, to avoid being around people I know and the embarrassment of failure). I tried to sell executive coaching services but I lacked the self-confidence needed to be successful.

Now God had my attention. I realized my dreadful spiritual condition and clearly saw myself for what I was: a shallow, proud, self-centered man. It is amazing how blind I was to who I was and how tragedy created such clarity. I lost 25 pounds and became clinically depressed. Upon seeing who I had become, I repented and sought out God. By God's grace, my wife stood by me, my family was supportive, and my relationship with my property development partner became stronger as we faced our adversity together with God's help. For the first time in my life, I was developing a relationship with God and meaningful relationships with others. I immediately connected with a men's group of believers that became my lifeline. I confessed my sins to the men and to anyone else who would listen. I discovered two things: 1) everyone was understanding and forgiving, and 2) I was not alone. I was amazed at how many others had dealt with much more challenging issues than mine—and who were surviving with God's help.

Over the next few years, I dedicated myself to daily Bible study and prayer. I sought opportunities to be around godly men and rededicated myself to taking care of my family. I listened to religious programming and podcasts for hours each week. Little by little, God transformed my mind, my soul, and my life. I would like to say that God restored my wealth as He did for Job. However, I am not Job and God chose not to restore my lost money, at least not yet, and maybe never will. It's no longer important. He did, however, arrange for me and my business partner to dispose of our property without any leftover debt and to avoid bankruptcy—no small feat, and one that we could not have orchestrated without God's help.

More importantly, he blessed me in many other ways. I have a stronger relationship with my wife than before, and I am closer to my children. God has also given me opportunities to serve by supporting other men in times of trouble. Additionally, I no longer obsess about the material things that used to be the very center of my life. I have a good job, giving me an opportunity to serve others. Most importantly, I now have a real relationship with God and complete trust in His power to help me through any situation. I now know that I can do all things through Him who strengthens me.

While I had not previously committed my story to paper, I have gone over the details in my mind many times. I promised God that I would tell my story, given the opportunity. Thanks for giving me the venue to write it down. God has been on my shoulder for almost six years now. Documenting this story was a natural thing to do.

As with you, I am tempted to let regret creep in. "If only, I'd..." And then I remember that if I had not gone through my trial by fire, I could not have grown spiritually to where I am now (and I have so much more growing to do). I could have lived my entire life with, at best, a superficial relationship with God, and at worst, eternally lost. I was so blessed to go through the trial although it has taken me a few years to see it that way. My relationship with God now is worth immeasurably more than anything I "lost."

DAY 17

A Man's Faith Perseveres

JOSEPH SAID TO his brothers, "I am Joseph! Is my father still living?" But his brothers were not able to answer him, because they were terrified at his presence.

Then Joseph said to his brothers, "Come close to me." When they had done so, he said, "I am your brother Joseph, the one you sold into Egypt! And now, do not be distressed and do not be angry with yourselves for selling me here, because it was to save lives that God sent me ahead of you. For two years now there has been famine in the land, and for the next five years there will not be plowing and reaping. But God sent me ahead of you to preserve for you a remnant on earth and to save your lives by a great deliverance. So then, it was not you who sent me here, but God. He made me father to Pharaoh, lord of his entire household and ruler of all Egypt.

(Gen. 45:3-8)

What if you were awakened in darkness and a bag was placed over your head. What if someone then tied your hands and removed you from your home along with your children and your wife, and then placed you in slavery for the next 20 years? What if someone framed you for a crime you did not commit? What if you were put into a prison and you were innocent? What if you were bullied at school, beaten, and left for dead and later no longer had the use of one eye? What if you were a soldier in a just war and you lost both of your legs defending your country? What if you were attacked by people at work who were eliminating their competition, and you lost your job because of their lies? What if you lost your child at childbirth? What if you lost your wife as well? What if you were born in a ghetto next to a rich community and each day you saw those around you hungry while others thrived?

There are men around you who hang onto a tiny thread of faith or have none at all because of how they view their circumstances or their experiences with life. There are also men around you who rise up out of the conditions of life only because of their faith.

While I know that these things are true, I do not know how I would react within the situations described above. My father died an alcoholic when I was young. I remember my mother hiding or throwing away the Jack Daniels' bottles. I remember his lack of intimacy with me. I remember the pain. I remember his no-shows at ball games. I remember choosing a business and then in a few months being near bankruptcy. I remember being attacked in a religious setting for reading words from the Bible with the passion I saw there. I remember being blamed for something I did not do. I remember falling to my knees in prayer over past mistakes that threatened my family's provision. These are parts of my journey. What are yours?

We all have different paths to walk in this world. Sometimes I forget about mine when I see the struggles of others. I know today I'm a better man for believing God could change me, and for trusting He would show up and intersect with my life. I am better because He did change me, and I can tell others about His power with an authentic belief born out of experience.

Here's what Peter Simon Barjona said 2000 years ago after He accepted Christ as His Lord and Savior: "Praise be to the God and Father of our Lord Jesus Christ! In his great mercy he has given us new birth into a living hope through the resurrection of Jesus Christ from the dead, and into an inheritance that can never perish, spoil or fade-kept in heaven for you, who through faith are shielded by God's power until the coming of the salvation that is ready to be *revealed in the last time. In this you greatly rejoice, though now for a little while you may have had to suffer grief in all kinds of trials. These have come so that your faith-of greater worth than gold, which perishes even though refined by fire—may be proved genuine and may result in praise, glory and honor when Jesus Christ is revealed"* (1 Pet. 1:3-7).

We are being refined by fire by the troubles we face in life. As our faith strengthens through these times, God uses us to help others in similar circumstances. Here's the way the Apostle Paul explains this: "Praise be to the God and Father of our Lord Jesus Christ, the Father of compassion and the God of all comfort, *who comforts us in all our troubles, so that we can comfort those in any trouble with the comfort we ourselves have received from God.* For just as the sufferings of Christ flow over into our lives, so also through Christ our comfort overflows" (2 Cor. 1:4).

God has crafted you for such as time as this. Hold onto your faith and rise up with Him. He does more with humble and grateful people than with the prideful or arrogant. Everything in a man's life depends on God. Believe this today and ask for Him to strengthen you and to show you the work He has for you. Whether in jail, the hospital, or in a comfy position, you have much to do for others and for His glory.

--- --- ---

A MAN OF FAITH PERSEVERES
(your thoughts and actions)

Please read the story written in Mark 9:14-29.

The man uses the word "if." What did that imply to Jesus? How did Jesus reply? What does the man immediately exclaim?

_____

_____

_____

_____

_____

We do not control God, nor does He operate within our time frames or desires. Some things in life we want Him to heal or solve now. They hurt us, or others, even to the point of death—like losing a son in a war. Please read Romans 4:18-25 and Matt. 26:34-42.

_____

_____

_____

_____

_____

As He approaches the cross, what does Jesus say about His soul?

As He falls to the ground in prayer, what does He pray? What does He realize?

Finally, what does He pray the second time? How will His example affect how you pray? Reconcile the prayer of Jesus with the words here. (James 1: 5-6)

Look at the cross, see Him hanging there without sin, FOR YOU, and take up your cross and follow Him.

DAY 18

Men Chosen to Lead

THE NEXT DAY Moses took his seat to serve as judge for the people, and they stood around him from morning till evening. When his father-in-law saw all that Moses was doing for the people, he said, "What is this you are doing for the people? Why do you alone sit as judge, while all these people stand around you from morning till evening?"

Moses answered him, "Because the people come to me to seek God's will. Whenever they have a dispute, it is brought to me, and I decide between the parties and inform them of God's decrees and laws."

Moses' father-in-law replied, "What you are doing is not good. You and these people who come to you will only wear yourselves out. The work is too heavy for you; you cannot handle it alone. Listen now to me and I will give you some advice, and may God be with you. You must be the people's representative before God and bring their disputes to him. Teach them the decrees and laws, and show them the way to live and the duties they are to perform. But select capable men from all the people–men who fear God, trustworthy men who hate dishonest gain–and appoint them as officials over thousands, hundreds, fifties and tens. Have them serve as judges for the people at all times, but have them bring every difficult case to you; the simple cases they can decide themselves. That will make your load lighter, because they will share it with you. If you do this and God so commands, you will be able to stand the strain, and all these people will go home satisfied."

(Ex. 18:13-23)

A team of people forms around a common mission and when they do, someone leads them to accomplish it. We see this cultural formation everywhere around us. In families, sports, business, nonprofits, and religious organizations, leaders coordinate the talents and actions of others. In doing so, they help maintain a right spirit as the organization achieves its objectives and reason for existence.

In some organizations the needs and number of people on the team increase, making it difficult for one man to perform leadership duties with effectiveness. Decisions and routines become more complex than one person can manage. At the same time, people need to be rerouted from unproductive and perhaps dangerous tendencies.

When these situations linger, the team members suffer from wasted time and inaction on important matters. This lack of leadership strength frustrates the team's ability to accomplish its objectives with efficiency and with a cooperative spirit. Also, no one confronts inappropriate behavior in a timely manner, and unless additional leaders are chosen, the team stops working together, loses members, or dissolves.

Godly men steward their own talents and, as leaders of missional groups, the talents of others to bring people to Jesus. They help people grow in loving God and others. All groups have a godly purpose in business, home or church. Godly men lead them to perform a function that shows the love of God toward the physical, emotional and spiritual needs of others. This becomes apparent by the sacrificial intent of an individual or team's service.

How effective are you at leading yourself?

Did you know that life at times becomes so complex that one man cannot handle his own stuff? Men need other men to listen to them. Men need other men to walk with them and pray with them. Men need other men for wisdom and advice. And while men do need other men, there is no better sounding board for a married man than his bride's intuition before God. She often sees wider and deeper into what surrounds any decision.

A man leads with courage.

A man seeks wise counsel.

A man chooses others to help him when he cannot do what needs to be done.

A man listens to his wife.

Here's what Solomon says:

"The way of a fool seems right to him, but a wise man listens to advice."

"Pride only breeds quarrels, but wisdom is found in those who take advice."

"Listen to advice and accept instruction, and in the end you will be wise."

"Like an archer who wounds at random is he who hires a fool or any passer-by."

"Though one may be overpowered, two can defend themselves. A cord of three strands is not quickly broken."

"A wife of noble character who can find? She is worth far more than rubies."

(Prov. 12:15; 13:10; 19:20; 26:10; Eccl. 4:12; Prov. 31:10)

When we choose people to help us as an individual or in our efforts as a leader, here are some important considerations.

§ Are they capable?
§ Do they have a reverential respect and love for God?
§ Are they trustworthy men who hate dishonesty?

~ ~ ~

MEN CHOSEN TO LEAD
(your thoughts and actions)

What are you doing that is not good, and for which good advice would be helpful?

_____

_____

_____

_____

_____

Who can mentor you or where can you get the advice you need? Decide when you will call them or go see them. Do not put this off. Make this a habit when you need counsel.

_____

_____

_____

_____

_____

It's been my misfortune (and at times ruin) in not heeding or asking for the advice of my godly bride who loves Jesus. I have found that she is blessed with a supernatural intuition. Realize that "she is your helpmate" given to you by God, and enrich your marriage and your decisions with her input.

_____

_____

_____

_____

_____

_____

Make yourself available to your children, family members, and others as a mentor in areas in which God has given you strength. Please write these areas down and pray that God uses you in service to others.

_____

_____

_____

_____

_____

_____

Remember, "Though one may be overpowered, two can defend themselves. A cord of three strands is not quickly broken" (Eccl. 4:12). Seek advice and do not live out life alone. Seek a brotherhood and fellowship of men bonded to each other and fighting the battles of life together._

DAY 19

Men Who Know the Truth

THEY GAVE MOSES this account: "We went into the land to which you sent us, and it does flow with milk and honey! Here is its fruit. But the people who live there are powerful, and the cities are fortified and very large. We even saw descendants of Anak there. The Amalekites live in the Negev; the Hittites, Jebusites and Amorites live in the hill country; and the Canaanites live near the sea and along the Jordan."

Then Caleb silenced the people before Moses and said, "We should go up and take possession of the land, for we can certainly do it." But the men who had gone up with him said, "We can't attack those people; they are stronger than we are."

And they spread among the Israelites a bad report about the land they had explored. They said, "The land we explored devours those living in it. All the people we saw there are of great size. We saw the Nephilim there (the descendants of Anak come from the Nephilim). We seemed like grasshoppers in our own eyes, and we looked the same to them."

That night all the people of the community raised their voices and wept aloud. All the Israelites grumbled against Moses and

Aaron, and the whole assembly said to them, "If only we had died in Egypt! Or in this desert! Why is the LORD bringing us to this land only to let us fall by the sword? Our wives and children will be taken as plunder. Wouldn't it be better for us to go back to Egypt?" And they said to each other, "We should choose a leader and go back to Egypt."

Then Moses and Aaron fell facedown in front of the whole Israelite assembly gathered there. Joshua son of Nun and Caleb son of Jephunneh, who were among those who had explored the land, tore their clothes and said to the entire Israelite assembly, "The land we passed through and explored is exceedingly good. If the LORD is pleased with us, he will lead us into that land, a land flowing with milk and honey, and will give it to us. Only do not rebel against the LORD. And do not be afraid of the people of the land, because we will swallow them up. Their protection is gone, but the LORD is with us. Do not be afraid of them."

(Num. 13:27-14:9)

When you look at certain geometric objects or drawings from different perspectives, they appear to change their shapes and morph into something else. What we see are simply optical illusions or graphic tricks created by how something is drawn. Our continued examination reveals hidden objects or another way to hold the picture in our minds.

In life, men observe the same situation and have a variety of opinions and reactions, especially when moving forward demands courage, determination, and faith in God. They see the same circumstances with contrasting outlooks and then talk and behave according to their perception. Why? Can you explain this with only the words optimism and pessimism?

What is true about your purpose and direction in life matters. What is true about the work you've been given to do matters. What is true about how God sees you matters. What is true about God matters. It's not what you think and feel that matters, it's what God says is true that matters. We will talk and behave according to what we think and feel is true. But is it true? Is it true?

Reread the Bible story above about Moses and the Israelites. Now, what was true?

— — —

Knowing the truth of God's promises first starts with faith in God—even a small amount. It also requires a belief that the Bible is accurate and true in all of the principles it teaches, because without the Bible, all we know about God and Jesus will be based on each person's feelings and thoughts.

So, learn from the stories in the Bible and associate with other men of God who are striving to grow and mature in Christ. Ask them to pray for you. Do not react to the first opinions of those around you. Get and test advice by praying, reading the Bible and looking for His words to mold you, and by listening to what the Spirit of God says to your conscience.

To know if something is true starts with faith and continues with a deepening relationship with Jesus that grows out of seeking Him in everything. Then faith during trials and times of testing increases your perseverance, changes your character, and produces hope, and hope does not disappoint us (see Romans 5 and James 1).

Who is God to you? What mission has He given you in your family, at your work, and in the world? If He gives you any task, He will give you what you need to do it to His glory and in service to others.

— — —

MEN WHO KNOW THE TRUTH
(your thoughts and actions)

What promises has God made concerning His people? Write at least 10 down, and if you need help, use your Bible.

Ask two other people to do the exercise above and then sit over some coffee and compare what you've written. Write down any promises that you did not include in your list.

Now, order your list 1-10 and write your list again with the most important promises listed first, then find these promises in the Bible and write down where they are located.

Which of these truths do you need to remember at this point in your life? How are your present behaviors and thoughts not in alignment with the truth? Write the most important 1-3 Bible verses you need to memorize and mediate on. Do this in the next week.

_____

_____

_____

_____

_____

_____

Each day the world displays messages that assault the words and promises of God and offer men an alternative "truth." Read the Bible. Pray. Get around those who know the truth. Overcome the dullness that occurs when the world bombards our minds with tantalizing substitutes and fearful fixations. Free yourself and protect your hearts and minds in Christ Jesus.

DAY 20

Men Follow Jesus Wholeheartedly

BUT BECAUSE MY servant Caleb has a different spirit and follows me wholeheartedly, I will bring him into the land he went to, and his descendants will inherit it. ...

The LORD'S anger was aroused that day and he swore this oath: "Because they have not followed me wholeheartedly, not one of the men twenty years old or more who came up out of Egypt will see the land I promised on oath to Abraham, Isaac and Jacob- not one except Caleb son of Jephunneh the Kenizzite and Joshua son of Nun, for they followed the LORD wholeheartedly."

"O LORD, God of Israel, there is no God like you in heaven above or on earth below-you who keep your covenant of love with your servants who continue wholeheartedly in your way.

The people rejoiced at the willing response of their leaders, for they had given freely and wholeheartedly to the LORD.

(Num. 14:24; 32:10; 1 Kings 8:23; 1 Chron. 29:9)

~ ~ ~

My grandfather's name on my mother's side of the family was John David Grant Isaacs. I loved being around him as a kid—early mornings to the lake for fishing, listening to stories of his life, or breakfast with eggs, redeye gravy, and biscuits. It was all good for he was a strong man, a patient man, and a provider. He worked hard all his life as a master carpenter until his death at 93 while putting in a fan standing on a ladder. He was reaching to a second story window when God took him home. My grandfather loved me.

Last night, with the power of the Internet and other's people's previous efforts, I looked down my grandfather's ancestral tree to England from one Isaac man to another, all the way to Brian Isaacs (born 1558—died 1636), and my mind drifted to these questions. Who were all these Issacs' men—from Brian, to James, Ralph, John, Samuel (Virginia), Samuel (Jr.), Godfrey, Godfrey (Jr.), Fielding, Samuel L, to my grandfather John David Grant and his daughter Nola Isaacs Cooper? What decisions did they make in what were short or long life spans? What beliefs did they pass on to the men in their families? How did they affect me and how did God interact with their stories? Did they stand strong with Jesus?

Somehow I'm here—alive today. They survived childbirth. They made a family. Now it's up to me. And, you're here with me too. So, it's up to you as well.

Where will you put your trust? Where will you put your heart—your whole heart? In the story of Caleb and in the last book of the Bible, a warning emerges about half-hearted men ... "I know your deeds, that you are neither cold nor hot. I wish you were either one or the other! So, because you are lukewarm—neither hot nor cold—I am about to spit you out of my mouth" (Rev. 3:15-16).

You know the good news of Jesus Christ. You are assured that He loves you and has a place for you in heaven. You also know that you are to pick up your cross and follow Him and that future generations may be blessed by your decision. It's an awesome love and an awesome responsibility that can begin for your children and your children's children just because of you.

It's the 21st century. The day begins. Men eat their breakfast or grab a $5 cup of coffee, and their cars race down the interstate. They once again arise to pursue their interests, and God pays close attention to what they chase after and in what manner. Men will make decisions today about what they will eat, how they will approach problems, and where they will place their faith. What they think and speak about, and who they follow, will affect their family and the culture around them. Their choices will affect the quality of life for boys and girls, both now and tomorrow.

(... be careful, and watch yourselves closely so that you do not forget the things your eyes have seen or let them slip from your heart as long as you live. Teach them to your children and to their children after them. Hear, O Israel: The LORD our God, the LORD is one. Love the LORD your God with all your heart and with all your soul and with all your strength. These commandments that I give you today are to be upon your hearts. Impress them on your children. Talk about them when you sit at home and when you walk along the road, when you lie down and when you get up." (Deut. 4:9; 6:4-7)

So, serve wholeheartedly, as if you were serving the Lord, not men (Eph. 6:7). Be enthusiastic in your faith and determined in the tasks that you receive from God. Show great interest in your relationship with Jesus and your spiritual life. Be aggressive toward God and allow God's Spirit to produce this "fruit" in your life: love, joy, peace, patience, kindness, goodness, faithfulness, gentleness, self-control (Gal. 5:22-23). Strive to grow and to be better as a man of God.

—— —— ——

MEN WHO FOLLOW JESUS WHOLEHEARTEDLY
(your thoughts and actions)

Are you all in? It's hard to set fire to the boat and push it off from shore. It's hard to give your best, but are you all in? Have you asked God to take it all?

_____

_____

_____

_____

_____

_____

What do you hold back from Him? Does your conscience remind you of an area of your life that you hold onto? Do you rationalize with yourself about it?

_____

_____

_____

_____

_____

What happens when you go to war with a man who isn't committed to his place in the line? How does that affect your safety and the mission you are given?

_____

_____

_____

_____

_____

What would happen if you were all in for Jesus, for God, and for being led by His Spirit? How would this affect your family, your work, and the believers you work with at your church?

_____

_____

_____

_____

_____

_____

Look for opportunities to tell stories about Jesus and His walk with you. Push hard into this day with all the effort and energy you can find for the benefit of others and the glory of God. Let others see your faith in God by your hard work, encouragement and concern for them. Be strong and courageous in Him.

"How great is the love the Father has lavished on us, that we should be called children of God! And that is what we are!"

1 John 3:1

A Man Moved by God

That We Should Be Called Children of God

MY LIFE WAS a lie. My deception wasn't constructed to gain something from others, but more to protect myself from others. During my early teenage years I was in a depression. My spirit had been severely damaged and I didn't really understand how I was damaged, nor did I understand how to heal myself. I had been physically and sexually abused by my Scout Master, and this somehow altered who I was. As a result, I sought out God in many places, but I found no solace in Him. However, I continued to walk forward with my eyes lifted up to Him, stumbling, falling, and deceiving myself, that I could overcome that wound on my own. I hid the truth from my parents and friends. I continued to pull myself up by my "boot straps", struggling through each day, wearing masks of kindness and patience. In reality, I was a seething, boiling caldron of pain and resentment inside. I would walk into a room full of friends and family, yet I felt so alone.

Early on, prior to marrying, I tried alcohol to soothe the pain. Then I tried self-help books and inspirational books. I sought God in the rules and obligations of the Mormon Church. I even served on a mission for the Mormon Church, and although I was a "successful" missionary, I cried daily in the bathroom as I struggled with my dual life. The path I was walking was a solitary one.

Returning from the mission field, I married a wonderful woman, hoping I could find joy in those familiar relationships. And although married and a father of five, I found very little joy in life. Then, I tried another way of healing myself, in the arms of another woman. Not just any woman, but a woman I had loved as a young man: my first love. And interestingly, as a young man I broke off the relationship because I was convinced I wasn't good enough for her. The self-loathing filtered everything I saw, so what I saw looked dark and unappealing.

When the truth of my indiscretion came to light, I was relieved and devastated. And although my marriage couldn't be saved, I finally opened up to God and others about my past. I realized that throughout my entire life, I had lived with the goal of pleasing others, hoping somehow I would fill the huge void in my heart through acts of kindness and service. Then, early one morning, as I studied the Bible with a friend, I read a verse that changed my life.

How great is the love the Father has lavished on us, that we should be called children of God! And that is what we are! The reason the world does not know us is that it did not know him.

(1 John 3:1)

In that moment, my life changed. I knew I was a Son of God. I knew He loved me and that was all I needed. I was healed internally and spiritually, in a way that all of the years of reading, missionary work and self-work never could. And although my abuse left a scar, it is no longer a gaping wound. I can feel the scar but it only reminds me of how evil exists in the world; that the only protection is God's love. Stealing a Steve Martin line, He was "all that I need(ed)".

When I finally opened up my life to others, sharing my pain and my deep sense of loss, my love for God grew. Now as I look back on my life, I am grateful for the special insights I have into the pain of others around me. I regret the pain I caused my family, but I try to honor them daily through my actions. I have been given a unique gift of seeing into the hearts of others—a special intuition. I call it "putting on my God glasses," filtering things as I hope God would and does. I am grateful for my brothers in Christ that continue to help me with the ongoing fight under God's flag.

~ ~ ~

In spite of the blessing of grace and forgiveness bestowed on me, even as I wrote, I was reminded of how the deceiver never sleeps and tries to push doubt in the face of truth. I felt such a struggle of not being worthy of His love.

DAY 21

Men Tell Stories

DO WHAT IS right and good in the LORD'S sight, so that it may go well with you and you may go in and take over the good land that the LORD promised on oath to your forefathers, thrusting out all your enemies before you, as the LORD said.

In the future, when your son asks you, "What is the meaning of the stipulations, decrees and laws the LORD our God has commanded you?" tell him: "We were slaves of Pharaoh in Egypt, but the LORD brought us out of Egypt with a mighty hand. Before our eyes the LORD sent miraculous signs and wonders–great and terrible–upon Egypt and Pharaoh and his whole household. But he brought us out from there to bring us in and give us the land that he promised on oath to our forefathers. The LORD commanded us to obey all these decrees and to fear the LORD our God, so that we might always prosper and be kept alive, as is the case today. And if we are careful to obey all this law before the LORD our God, as he has commanded us, that will be our righteousness."

(Deut. 6:18-25)

Everyone loves a good story. The author John Eldridge tells us that the best ones stir our hearts as we live out their adventures, fight in their battles, and ultimately rescue the people involved. We spend billions of dollars making and viewing movies with this typical design pattern: Once upon a time...and every day the people were experiencing... until one day something changed... and because of this, the tension and conflict heightened...until finally people found a way past it ...and ever since that day, they live a new life.

In the beginning, God created the heavens and the earth, the trees, the animals, man and then woman. He put Adam and Eve in the garden to care for it and to enjoy all of it except the fruit of one tree, which if eaten would cause them to die. Each day the earth's first man and woman lived to love God and each other. They were perfectly at peace only knowing the good things of the garden's beauty and the love relationship they lived in it.

Until one day, a crafty serpent approached them and told them that God had lied. Adam and Eve believed him instead of God, and they touched and ate the forbidden fruit. Because of this, their eyes were opened to good and evil and they spiritually and physically began to die. God then banished them from the garden and sent them to work in a decaying world of thorns and thistles.

The generations after them wandered about the earth looking for significance, comfort, and control to replace their lost spirituality and purpose. Love and intimacy were blocked by evil thoughts. A peaceful life turned into one of fear and fighting.

This continued for hundreds of years until God persevered in His love with a remnant of one nation, Israel. Through His Son, He brought His people back into His arms and saved them. You see, God so loved the world that He gave his one and only Son, that whoever believes in Him shall not perish but have eternal life (John 3:16).

Ever since that day, many people are being saved and reborn spiritually by their faith in Him.

Men, you have a story of salvation and a changed life. In the future, when someone asks, tell it. Tell it to your sons and daughters. Allow them to hear about your life before and after Jesus. Let them know about your love relationship with the Messiah. Encourage them with your adventure, the battles in it, and your ultimate escape. Let them see your new life with its peace and assurance, and then let them know who saved you and how it occurred. "But do this with gentleness and respect." (1 Peter 3:15)

MEN TELL STORIES
(your thoughts and actions)

Have you ever thought about how your life intersects with the greatest story ever told and that you have a warrior's place in its battle lines and victories? Think about your story up to now. What parts or roles have you played in the story? Describe your character.

_____

_____

_____

_____

_____

_____

Have you been in the wings watching, oblivious of the play on the stage, playing with your toys, doing the wrong things in secret places, or have you been in the battle fighting with men and women for one side or the other?

_____

_____

_____

_____

_____

_____

How has God written a new storyline for you? How has that made all the difference? When did it happen or has it been happening in degrees over the years? Or, are you in the wings avoiding a faithful walk and dependence on His leading?

Please write your story in less than 1000 words and follow this outline. Once upon a time, you were doing this or that...and every day you were experiencing...until one day or over many days, something changed... and because of this, the tension and conflict heightened in your life... until finally after this and that, you found a way past it with God ...and ever since that day (or those days), your life has changed in these (wonderful) ways because of Him.

Tell your story and how faith in God has brought you to a new and better place and how each morning you walk onto its stage and into life's battles with purpose and significance and victory.

Today, Jesus is your righteousness. He has brought salvation to a dying world. He is your everlasting hope.

He is the reason for any season.

DAY 22

Men Face Goliath

DAVID, A SHEPHERD boy destined to be a king, said to Saul, "Let no one lose heart on account of this Philistine; your servant will go and fight him."

— — —

Then he took his staff in his hand, chose five smooth stones from the stream, put them in the pouch of his shepherd's bag and, with his sling in his hand, approached the Philistine. Meanwhile, the Philistine, with his shield bearer in front of him, kept coming closer to David.

He looked David over and saw that he was only a boy, ruddy and handsome, and he despised him. He said to David, "Am I a dog, that you come at me with sticks?" And the Philistine cursed David by his gods. "Come here," he said, "and I'll give your flesh to the birds of the air and the beasts of the field!"

David said to the Philistine, "You come against me with sword and spear and javelin, but I come against you in the name of the LORD Almighty, the God of the armies of Israel, whom you have defied. This day the LORD will hand you over to me, and I'll strike you down and cut off your head. Today I will give the carcasses of the Philistine army to the birds of the air and the beasts of the earth, and the whole world will know that there is a God in Israel. All those gathered here will know that it is not by sword or spear that the LORD saves; for the battle is the LORD'S, and he will give all of you into our hands."

As the Philistine moved closer to attack him, David ran quickly toward the battle line to meet him. Reaching into his bag and taking out a stone, he slung it and struck the Philistine on the forehead. The stone sank into his forehead, and he fell facedown on the ground.

So David triumphed over the Philistine with a sling and a stone; without a sword in his hand, He struck down the Philistine and killed him. David ran and stood over him. He took hold of the Philistine's sword and drew it from the scabbard. After he killed him, he cut off his head with the sword. When the Philistines saw that their hero was dead, they turned and ran.

(1 Sam. 17:32, 40-51)

Men find that Goliaths come in all shapes, sizes and disguises. I remember a book by Dr. Robert Schuller written several years ago entitled *Goliath*. He wrote about a man's encounter with Goliath at unanticipated times in his life. For him, one of those times included his daughter's loss of a leg in a car accident. There were other times as well. Dr. Schuller did not give a reason for why those fearful encounters occurred, but he did spread hope with his personal understanding of faith and God's promises to bring us peace and power in spite of the circumstances we face. One of his other books was entitled: *Tough Times Never Last, but Tough People Do.*

For men, our giants come in many different disguises; an attack of a close friend, a spouse's infidelity, or the loss of a job. A challenge to your manhood and your walk with Jesus stands in your way in one form or another. Perhaps, you have a heart attack or you're diagnosed with cancer. Maybe you lose a child, or your bride of 30 years dies.

Sometimes this giant brings a challenge to a country, a family, or a team in a company, and someone must rise up to meet him. The giant was Hitler in Germany and it was Goliath thousands of years ago. Someone must lead. Someone must know and remind the others that God will prevail one way or another.

Will you face the fear?

Will you fight?

Will you have the hard conversations?

Will you tell the truth?

Will you face off Goliath?

Will you keep moving against the enemy?

Will you be the one to die for what is right?

WILL YOU CLING TO AND DEPEND ON GOD?

~ ~ ~

God knows you will face Goliath in this world. He realizes tough moments will test your faith with pain, anxiety or uncertainty. You will face danger and disappointments. You will hear lies. You will experience situations that discourage you. A dark force seeking to rule in this world will also try and take you down and even kill you, or he will work to make you ineffective for those around you. He did in the beginning, and he roams around looking to do so today.

Remember these words from heroes of old as they faced their moments of truth:

"He took courage." (King Asa: 2 Chr. 15:8)

"Act with courage." (King Jehoshaphat: 2 Chr. 19:11)

"Take courage and do it." (Ezra a High Priest of Israel: Ezra 10:4)

"Be on your guard; stand firm in the faith; be men of courage; be strong." Paul: 1 Cor. 16:13)

"Take courage! It is I. Don't be afraid." (Jesus: Matt: 14:27; Mark 6:50; Acts 23:11)

～ ～ ～

MEN FACE GOLIATH
(your thoughts and actions)

Read 2 Chron. 15:1-15. It's a great story about how one man, Asariah, was moved by God's Spirit to face off a king (King Asa) with the truth during a time when nations were at war. It occured at a time when the people of Israel were experiencing great distress.

_____

_____

_____

_____

_____

What does Asariah tell King Asa and all the people?

_____

_____

_____

_____

In their distress, what did they do and what happened?

_____

_____

_____

_____

When he tells them to "be _____ and
do not _____," what does he say about their work?

_____
_____
_____
_____
_____
_____

How does the story end? (verse 15)

_____
_____
_____
_____
_____

Goliath appears in many forms and strikes at the heart of a man.

"Be on your guard; stand firm in the faith; be men of courage; be strong." (Paul: 1 Cor. 16:13)

DAY 23

A Man's Cave

THAT DAY, DAVID fled from Saul and went to Achish king of Gath. But the servants of Achish said to him, "Isn't this David, the king of the land? Isn't he the one they sing about in their dances: "'Saul has slain his thousands, and David his tens of thousands'?"

David took these words to heart and was very much afraid of Achish king of Gath. So he pretended to be insane in their presence; and while he was in their hands he acted like a madman, making marks on the doors of the gate and letting saliva run down his beard.

Achish said to his servants, "Look at the man! He is insane! Why bring him to me? Am I so short of madmen that you have to bring this fellow here to carry on like this in front of me? Must this man come into my house?"

David left Gath and escaped to the cave of Adullam. When his brothers and his father's household heard about it, they went down to him there.

All those who were in distress or in debt or discontented gathered around him, and he became their leader. About four hundred men were with him.

From there, David went to Mizpah in Moab and said to the king of Moab, "Would you let my father and mother come and stay with you until I learn what God will do for me??

(1 Sam. 21:10-22:3)

- - -

Where do men flee to get away from the stress and anxiety of cutting through the thorns and thistles of this world? Some run to women—real ones or digital ones on the internet. Others immerse themselves in work, exercise, hobbies, fishing, hunting, sports, politics, or talk radio.

What is a man cave? It's a place a man maintains and reserves for his escape tools or toys. It could be a fancy entertainment den with a bar, flat screen television and theatre seating. Or, it could simply be a garage, a barn, a basement room or an office in the home. It could even be a fishing stream or a seat on a riding lawnmower. Whatever it is, there you will find a place where a man can insulate himself with memorabilia, hobbies, or reading material just for him. It's a place of pleasure. It's a place of work. Or, it's both.

But where does a man go when his man cave does not provide what he needs to fill his heart with faith and courage? Where does he go when he needs someone to lift him from the distress he feels? Where does he go when he has no more answers for the debt he owes either for his sins or for his financial condition? Where does he go to change his discontentment into gratefulness and peace despite his circumstances as he waits on God's movement in his life? Where does he go to find the power to change his habits? Where does he go to grow as a man of God and to learn what God will do for him? Where does he go to find REAL relief?

Now that's a different kind of man cave—the kind that David and a gathering of 400 men escaped to in "David left Gath and escaped to the cave of Adullam. All those who were in distress or in debt or discontented gathered around him, and he became their leader. About four hundred men were with him" (1 Sam. 22:1-2).

~ ~ ~

MEN'S GATHERING

Nine years ago, a few men gathered in the mountains of East Tennessee, because they recognized something was missing in their lives, and they expected to learn what God would do for them. When they did, some amazing stuff happened, and men:

- § Who were near suicide found hope and today live a life without torment.
- § Found real healing for the wounds of life.
- § Who had lost their families because of sin, turned in a new direction and regained them.
- § Turned from internet fantasy to manhood and real commitment.
- § Found meaning and purpose in life.
- § Found hope and encouragement and answers for the next step in their life.
- § Simply and profoundly found the definition of a man and the power to live it.
- § Learned how to love their wives deeper and wider than ever before.
- § Found Jesus, a relationship with the Son of God, for the first time in their lives.

During Men's Gatherings held in the Fall and Spring, men see a great work of God. They learn to reject passivity, accept responsibility, lead courageously, and invest in things that last forever. Lives change. Families are sewn back together, and good ones are made even stronger. Men grow better—not perfect—BETTER. You can too!

Today, young men, ages 18-35, who attend these semiannual gatherings, do or do not go to church or have a relationship with God. They come from all kinds of denominations and levels of faith or no faith. At these Gatherings of men, God forges a safe place with authentic and real talk.

Solomon, the wisest man who has ever lived, said this, "As iron sharpens iron, so one man sharpens another" (Prov. 27:17).

If you cannot come to a Men's Gathering in Tennessee, what do you do? Look around for a man of God—a Jesus lover. If you look for one, you will find one. Ask him to gather with you for the purpose of Bible discussion and prayer around what distresses you or steals your contentment. Ask him to help you find what God will do for you. Later, if God directs you, grow this group of men with one single purpose, "Finding what God will do for you as men who love Jesus."

Finally, if you have not already, search for a body of people who follow Jesus. Look for authenticity not perfection. Look for men who love Jesus, each other, and the world around them. Reject passivity and join in what they do with a servant-hearted mindset.

God has already done something wonderful for you in Jesus Christ. Believe in Him. His promise and presence is available now and forever.

A MAN'S CAVE
(your thoughts and actions)

Where do you go when you are afraid, or discontented or want to escape—when you want to think and pray and wait on an answer from God? Choose a place and do this.

_____

_____

_____

_____

_____

Do you have a group of men that you meet with? If not, find one and then two. Write down the names of men that you know love Jesus. It does not matter how old or young they are. Search them out, connect with them and seek God.

_____

_____

_____

_____

If you are in distress, in debt, or discontented, seek God to see what God will do for you. Fall to your knees. Many strong men in Bible stories did this.

_____

_____

_____

_____

When has God last moved your heart, changed your direction or given you peace? He waits for your approach, your cry and your petition. You are His son.

Rejoice in the Lord always. I will say it again: Rejoice! Let your gentleness be evident to all. The Lord is near. Do not be anxious about anything, but in everything, by prayer and petition, with thanksgiving, present your requests to God. And the peace of God, which transcends all understanding, will guard your hearts and your minds in Christ Jesus. (Phil. 4:4-7)

A Man's Big Decisions

IN THE SPRING, at the time when kings go off to war, David sent Joab out with the king's men and the whole Israelite army. They destroyed the Ammonites and besieged Rabbah. But David remained in Jerusalem. One evening David got up from his bed and walked around on the roof of the palace. From the roof he saw a woman bathing. The woman was very beautiful, and David sent someone to find out about her. The man said, "Isn't this Bathsheba, the daughter of Eliam and the wife of Uriah the Hittite?" Then David sent messengers to get her. She came to him, and he slept with her. (She had purified herself from her uncleanness.) Then she went back home.

In the morning, David wrote a letter to Joab and sent it with Uriah. In it he wrote, "Put Uriah in the front line where the fighting is fiercest. Then withdraw from him so he will be struck down and die." So while Joab had the city under siege, he put Uriah at a place where he knew the strongest defenders were. When the men of the city came out and fought against Joab, some of the men in David's army fell; moreover, Uriah the Hittite died.

When Uriah's wife heard that her husband was dead, she mourned for him. After the time of mourning was over, David had her brought to his house, and she became his wife and bore him a son. But the thing David had done displeased the LORD.

(2 Sam. 11:1-4, 14-17, 26-27)

Years ago, Jan Carlson used the words "moments of truth" to describe each contact an employee of Scandinavian Airlines had with a customer. These important moments occurred when a decision was made to treat a customer in a particular manner. While all of them had a cumulative effect on the reputation of the airline, some of these decisions he called "critical moments of truth." What was done around these critical and more important times caused far lasting effects unrealized at the time and were either helpful or detrimental to the company far into the future.

One decision can create a disastrous change in a man's life. Sometimes this impacts a family, a company, and even a country for years. As my friend Brian often says, "We are all one eyelash from making a big and very bad decision." In the newspapers and within our circle of friends, we see men:

§ Caught with women other than their wives.
§ Lie as politicians, CEOs, salespeople, or husbands.
§ Steal money from their company's customers.
§ Sell products that cannot live up to their promises.
§ Destroy relationships for power, money, or pleasure.
§ Drink, text, and cause accidents that harm others.

One small movement can lead to another and then another. Then you make the Big Decision—the one from which there is no quick recovery—and life changes forever for you and for those you affected. So, "Be sober, be vigilant; because your adversary the devil, as a roaring lion, walketh about, seeking whom he may devour" (1Peter 5:6 KJV).

Being vigilant means being alert and watchful and guarded against what the enemy uses to lure you into destruction. The small moments before the critical decision may seem insignificant, but they lead to one more step toward a big decision...and one that seems smaller because of the steps before it. Each bad decision becomes just one more foothold or point of progress away from a man's integrity before God and other men.

The Bible explains that living without God hardens the heart, and then, "Having lost all sensitivity, they have given themselves over to sensuality so as to indulge in every kind of impurity, with a continual lust for more" (Eph 4:19).

One small step at a time causes a man to lose sensitivity to what is right and leads to more and more, until finally a man faces the Big Decision. The Bible warns, "do not give the devil a foothold" (Eph. 4:27).

Men of God listen to the warnings that occur in their hearts before the small steps, and they walk away from those moments. Men of God throw themselves into the battles God gives them to fight with other men. They do not remain at home. They do not become lukewarm and passive to joining others in the great adventure. They pursue a living faith.

Men of God realize that women represent one of the biggest challenges and finest pleasures within God's kingdom. Respecting, honoring and protecting them keeps a man safe from a very bad decision. Loving them as their very own sisters and daughters helps men think of them with greater purity.

Loving wives as brides and as soul mates for life also helps strengthen our minds as we work hard at our relationships. Men of God learn to find their significance, comfort, and power in God and not in women, money, or control over their environment. Women do not become a prize to win but a partner in the great adventure, the battles of life, and in the rescue of people along the way.

Now, get your heads on straight and look in the direction God gives you. Get into battle gear today. Put on the "full armor of God, so when the day of evil comes, you may be able to stand your ground, and after you have done everything, stand. Stand firm then with the belt of truth buckled around your waist, with the breast-plate of righteousness in place, and with your feet fitted with the readiness that comes from the gospel of peace. In addition to all this, take up the shield of faith, with which you can extinguish all the flaming arrows of the evil one. Take the helmet of salvation and the sword of the Spirit, which is the word of God. And pray in the Spirit on all occasions with all kinds of prayers and requests" (Eph. 6:11-18).

A MAN'S BIG DECISION
(your thoughts and actions)

What small decisions today are dulling or moving you away from your relationship with Jesus?

What big decisions have you made that have changed the quality of your relationship with God and with those important to you?

Have you been moved to the point of great sorrow over bad decisions in your life, and have they caused you to pick yourself up out of the resulting chaos and drag yourself in God's direction?

Even if you have not, other men have made decisions with lasting and negative impact. Have you been moved by the grace of God and His protection over you that now you can turn to those men in trouble and offer God's mercy and encouragement?

Think about why and how you love Jesus and how to love those around you. And if you have made a bad decision or more than one in your life, now is the time to turn and learn about the armor prepared for the rest of the battles before you. Make the life ahead better. You may suffer the consequences of bad decisions throughout your life in various ways, but you can experience the joy and peace of Jesus Christ and the improvement He brings. I've seen this happen.

You do have "What It Takes"—Jesus!

"In the spring, at the time when kings go off to war ..."

2 Samuel 11:1

A Man Moved by God

Acknowledge Him in All My Ways

LIKE DAVID IN the Bible, I had risen in business to control a significant amount of money and territory and power. The years of hard work had paid off and I was in charge of my life. I did what I wanted with my money and my relationships, and I did it without paying attention to what God desired of me.

The story of Bathsheeba is especially dear to me because I allowed a woman to take refuge with me from her long-term boyfriend after they had gotten into a serious quarrel. Her boyfriend (who I considered a friend and who had moved to Colorado with her to help me open a new territory) was more or less sent to the front lines to be eliminated. He was asked to leave the territory within a year due to "unethical behavior" that was questionable, at best.

Meanwhile, I took her into my home and she decided to stay with me. Since those days, trouble has followed me closer than ever before, and I'm not really speaking of her. My trouble with her came after everything else fell apart, but I'm convinced now that she was never in the marriage for true love. She's made that abundantly clear in that she "likes" me as a person, but just doesn't love me.

When I was "King" she liked me a lot more, obviously. I supposed it's not the "King's" business anymore.

When I read the messages in this book about David, I realized that an author can quote only so much, but I was shocked to see the part left out of the story where God takes David's first-born son because of the magnitude of his sin. I have recently wondered what my punishment was meant to be, and if I have weathered the storm or if there is more to come.

Financially, I have lost everything that I ever earned or saved even down to my Rolex wristwatch, which went toward a final payment necessary to close on the short sale of my home in Denver. I moved from a Hummer to a beat up old car and from a high rise Penthouse condo overlooking the ski slopes to a small apartment in an area where poor folks walk to the convenience store (seemingly to buy drug paraphernalia and lottery tickets).

That said, I see all of these things as somewhat of a cleansing of my own sins, and a necessary reality check for me to relearn how so many people actually live. I had lost touch with reality and with the struggles of every day people, and I'm truly very glad to become reacquainted with their challenges, which are now my own.

Overcoming those obstacles isn't as easy as I "THE GREAT CHARLATAN" had once stood before many and professed. "Why, I would just shoot right to the top if I were there," I must have said at one time or another. It isn't that easy.

Like David, I did get a child (and then another one) that was very special as the end result. I am very thankful for that, in spite of my failures and my decisions.

My armor is on and it's beat all to hell, but I'm still wearing it and it obviously works. Without it I would have already fallen. Like David, I am strong in faith and will stand in God's name looking forward. I have a strong feeling that great things will begin to start happening. They already have in many ways, and I'm grateful for those blessings.

Today, my life (although challenging much of the time) has been enriched with new blessings, understandings and beliefs that benefit me more so than monetarily. I have begun to learn to put my faith in the Lord with regard to my well being. Before, I had no faith that things would be OK unless I was the one to make it happen. I had to burn to the ground to realize that I could not do it alone before my eyes and ears were opened to God's messages.

Now, I am slowly but surely starting to realize that my well being is God's will, and that selfish matters should not be important to me. Rather, I have learned to ask for abilities to be used for specific purposes that might please God, and in doing so have found that my own well-being is interconnected with doing God's will. Again, I am learning these things to be true and I do not profess to have a quick answer or solution to my challenges or those of others. That is God's work, and that is what I'm learning.

Mighty Men!

THESE ARE THE names of David's mighty men: Josheb-Basshebeth, a Tahkemonite, was chief of the Three; he raised his spear against eight hundred men, whom he killed in one encounter.

Next to him was Eleazar son of Dodai the Ahohite. As one of the three mighty men, he was with David when they taunted the Philistines gathered [at Pas Dammim] for battle. Then the men of Israel retreated, but he stood his ground and struck down the Philistines till his hand grew tired and froze to the sword. The LORD brought about a great victory that day. The troops returned to Eleazar, but only to strip the dead.

Next to him was Shammah son of Agee the Hararite. When the Philistines banded together at a place where there was a field full of lentils, Israel's troops fled from them. But Shammah took his stand in the middle of the field. He defended it and struck the Philistines down, and the LORD brought about a great victory.

Abishai the brother of Joab son of Zeruiah was chief of the Three. He raised his spear against three hundred men, whom he killed, and so he became as famous as the Three. Was he not held in greater honor than the Three? He became their commander, even though he was not included among them.

Benaiah son of Jehoiada was a valiant fighter from Kabzeel, who performed great exploits. He struck down two of Moab's best men. He also went down into a pit on a snowy day and killed a lion. And he struck down a huge Egyptian. Although the Egyptian had a spear in his hand, Benaiah went against him with a club. He snatched the spear from the Egyptian's hand and killed him with his own spear.

Such were the exploits of Benaiah son of Jehoiada; he too was as famous as the three mighty men. He was held in greater honor than any of the Thirty, but he was not included among the Three. And David put him in charge of his bodyguard.

(2 Sam. 23:8-12; 1 Chron. 11:20-25)

Around the world, men of all ages stand in their bathrooms and admire their mighty physiques. They check their mirror to see if they've still got what it takes to compete as a man. A couple of poses, an investigation of danger areas, a lift to their chests and they convince themselves. They convince themselves that their muscle masses have tone and strength beyond reality.

Where do you go that you see powerful men in feats of physical excellence? When I grew up, I absorbed every new Superman and Green Lantern comic book I could find. I loved to sit, look at the pictures, and enter a world in which a hero could fly to someone's rescue. X-ray vision and the ability to stop a rifle's discharge with a bulletproof body were super cool. Occasionally, I would see a news story about a man lifting a car. The only other strong men I can think of back then were Green Berets and Army Rangers, and my grandfather (but he was old).

Today, we see Olympic athletes lift hundreds of pounds, while cable television takes us to the Highlands to see a man in kilts throwing logs during the Scottish games. In many cities, we pay to see cage fighters throw, kick, and pin their opponents until one yields and taps out. We also watch pro wrestling (which I think is more of a staged dance); and, of course, Monday Night Football and the NFL. In all of these, men do appear powerful and strong; yet, I've never heard of one man with a spear killing 800 men in one encounter—except maybe in video games the youth play on their computers (their version of yesterday's Flash Gordon).

When the money changers extorted money from those in the temple while selling their lambs and doves, Jesus, with focused intent, made a whip. He then walked to the temple and turned over their tables and whipped the beasts and people from the temple. He called the ruling Pharisees whitewashed tombs and hypocrites to their faces. In the end, their lies and politics maneuvered Him to the cross.

The Lion of Judah went to the cross as the Lamb of God.

Physical strength has its uses and those with guns increase their power to defend and take. But, what does Jesus mean when he says, "From the days of John the Baptist until now, the kingdom of heaven has been forcefully advancing, and forceful men lay hold of it" (Matt. 11:12)?

3 QUESTIONS

§ What is the kingdom of heaven?
§ How does the kingdom of heaven forcefully advance?
§ What does force look like in a man of God?

The Jews thought the Messiah would come and reunite them one last time as their earthly king. They believed he would take them out of bondage by force and into an everlasting kingdom on earth. They did not realize that the Messiah would be born in a manger, live a life of love, and then die on a cross to save all of humanity from sin. Instead of a kingdom on earth, the power of His life and death brought redemption and revolution into the hearts of men. The kingdom of heaven is simply the Spirit of God working in and through newly created and reborn people, and upon the world.

Since the death and resurrection of Jesus, men of God have been ambassadors of Christ and ministers of His reconciliation, the reuniting of God with His created people. Wow! We are in the last battles of the great adventure started thousands of years ago. In Revelation, the last book of the Bible, John the apostle says, "We win—the forces of evil lose!" Now, believers get up each day to spread the good news of His grace and to live as children of God, saved and free of condemnation, serving those around them in love. Each day their hearts are becoming more like Christ's as the power of His Spirit changes them in their inmost parts.

The force of our message displays itself in our changed condition before a watching world. They see us serve the poor. They see us love each other. They see us find peace in difficult situations. They see the evidence of faith in our joy and love. They hear us talk about our hope in God. They feel our love as we comfort them and listen to their heartaches and tend their wounds. They see us offer friendship and encouragement. They see our self-control and patience, our kindness and gentleness, our goodness and faithfulness. They see imperfect, humble, God-fearing and God-loving people who love others as they would love themselves.

"For physical training is of some value, but godliness has value for all things, holding promise for both the present life and the life to come." (1 Tim. 4:8)

I write to you, young men, because you are strong, and the word of God lives in you, and you have overcome the evil one. (1 John 2:14)

"And I heard a loud voice from the throne saying, ""Now the dwelling of God is with men, and he will live with them. They will be his people, and God himself will be with them and be their God."" (Rev. 21:3)

MIGHTY MEN
(your thoughts and actions)

Have you ever thought of yourself as a mighty man? Can a farmer be a mighty man? What about a laborer or an accountant? Today, in the last days, after the death and resurrection of Jesus, what does a "mighty man" look like to you?

_____

_____

_____

_____

_____

_____

What does it mean to be a man of honor?

_____

_____

_____

_____

_____

How does one man find favor with God and men?

_____

_____

_____

_____

_____

Be strong and courageous. Protect those around you. Advance God's kingdom with force, at home and at work and in all places, and these things will be advanced. Look up Galatians 5:18, 22-25. Write the "fruit of the Spirit" listed there on a 3x5 card and carry it with you. Pray for these as you find yourself in various life situations.

_____

_____

_____

_____

_____

_____

Because of Jesus, "Glory to God in the highest, and on earth peace to men on whom His favor rests" (Luke 2:14).

Now, go and serve others and glorify your Father in the name of the Son of God! Leave your play stations and be mighty men. The devil still roams and the world needs you!

DAY 26

Men Chase What Lasts!

AT GIBEON THE LORD appeared to Solomon during the night in a dream, and God said, "Ask for whatever you want me to give you." Solomon answered, "You have shown great kindness to your servant, my father David, because he was faithful to you and righteous and upright in heart. You have continued this great kindness to him and have given him a son to sit on his throne this very day."

"Now, O LORD my God, you have made your servant king in place of my father David. But I am only a little child and do not know how to carry out my duties. Your servant is here among the people you have chosen, a great people, too numerous to count or number. So give your servant a discerning heart to govern your people and to distinguish between right and wrong. For who is able to govern this great people of yours?"

The Lord was pleased that Solomon had asked for this. So God said to him, "Since you have asked for this and not for long life or wealth for yourself, nor have asked for the death of your enemies but for discernment in administering justice, I will do what you have asked. I will give you a wise and discerning heart, so that there will never have been anyone like you, nor will there ever be. Moreover, I will give you what you have not asked for–both riches and honor–so that in your lifetime you will have no equal among kings. And if you walk in my ways and obey my statutes and commands as David your father did, I will give you a long life."

(1 Kings 3:5-14)

~ ~ ~

Early in the morning, when they first rise from sleeping, men stand up and shake their heads. They stumble, then walk. Their eyes blink open in the light from the bathroom. Their heads clear. They think about the day's obligations. As the minutes pass and the day begins to unfold before them, they arrange as much time as possible around what they want. This means somehow gaining or maintaining control through acquisition or politics—i.e. getting something they desire. Or, they strive to find significance in their work or by who recognizes them. Some look for pleasure from what they enjoy, significance, power, acclaim, or a sense of conquest. They even may use a woman to help obtain these things. Anxieties begin to occur when something threatens their possessions. This state can carry over and keep them fearful and worried for weeks. The end result of this is bitterness, loneliness and despair, because everything they acquire is meaningless and empty vanity.

The more men accumulate, the more they have to manage and keep safe from loss. One thing breaks down and multiple things escalate the points of control necessary to keep it all spinning.

The more men need approval, the more people they have to satisfy to keep their image intact and unstained. If one person doesn't like them, and when faced with disapproval or a failure to perform, men look for a place, a person, or something that will help them mask their uncertainty.

This need for a "fix" results in decreased sensitivity towards others even intimacy with those they should love most, and ultimately in lost relationships. One more time, once more, another, they need another and it's never enough.

All of it for nothing. Later, someone else dresses you up and places you in a coffin. They walk around in your house. They use your things. They break them. They sell them. They throw the things you trusted to fill your needs and satisfy your wants away, while you lay in a pine box. The dirt spreads over the top of your coffin one shovel full after another, crawling up and over the side until the ground is level and your container of rest is buried and out of sight.

No one remembers. No one cares. You didn't care, so they don't. It all burns up and is thrown in with you—into the blackness of the dirt.

"Meaningless! Meaningless!" says the teacher. "Utterly meaningless! Everything is meaningless.What does man gain from all his labor at which he toils under the sun? Generations come and generations go, but the earth remains forever. The sun rises and the sun sets, and hurries back to where it rises. There is no remembrance of men of old, and even those who are yet to come will not be remembered by those who follow. (Eccl. 1: 2-5,11)

— — —

Turn and look at Him. He hangs there. Kneel and place your face on the ground. He has risen.

Cry out and give Him your life. Turn and love the ones He gives you to love. Turn and love your bride. Turn and love your parents. Turn and love your brother and your sister and your friends. Turn and love your employees. Turn and love the unlovely. Turn and love.

What remains? "Faith, hope, and love. But the greatest of these is love." (1 Cor. 13:13)

What is God saying to your heart? Who do you need to go to and ask forgiveness? Who do you need to call? Who do you need to visit? Who will you have lunch with and why? Who needs you to sit with them, listen to them, father them, or help them? Who needs encouragement, mentoring, food or love?

What does God want you to stop holding on to? What idol does he want you to turn from? What does God need to change in you for you to be a better man? Let Him do it. Let Him make you better, because joy will follow, and not just for you. Lives will change. People will be saved. Generations will be blessed.

And when the dirt crawls up the side of that wooden box, you will not be there! You will be smiling forever in a place that will be so beautiful and peaceful that you cannot describe it.

MEN CHASE WHAT LASTS
(your thoughts and actions)

Please find some quiet time, pray and write answers to these questions.

What does God want you to stop holding on to? What idol does he want you to turn from?

_____

_____

_____

_____

_____

_____

What does God need to change in your heart for you to be a better man?

_____

_____

_____

_____

_____

Give all of it up. Hold onto your faith. Hold onto the courage that comes from faith. Hold onto a life with Jesus that comes with faith. Love God. Love others.

Rebuilding Intimacy—Part III!

⟨⁓⟩

THE MAN SAID, "This is now bone of my bones and flesh of my flesh; she shall be called 'woman,' for she was taken out of man."

For this reason a man will leave his father and mother and be united to his wife, and they will become one flesh.

The man and his wife were both naked, and they felt no shame.

(Gen. 2:23-25)

How beautiful you are, my darling! Oh, how beautiful! Your eyes behind your veil are doves. Your hair is like a flock of goats descending from Mount Gilead. Your teeth are like a flock of sheep just shorn, coming up from the washing. Each has its twin; not one of them is alone.

Your lips are like a scarlet ribbon; your mouth is lovely. Your temples behind your veil are like the halves of a pomegranate.

Your neck is like the tower of David, built with elegance; on it hang a thousand shields, all of them shields of warriors. Your two breasts are like two fawns, like twin fawns of a gazelle that browse among the lilies. Until the day breaks and the shadows flee, I will go to the mountain of myrrh and to the hill of incense.

All beautiful you are, my darling; there is no flaw in you.

(Song 4:1-7)

This is what the LORD says: 'You say about this place, "It is a desolate waste, without men or animals." Yet in the towns of Judah and the streets of Jerusalem that are deserted, inhabited by neither men nor animals, there will be heard once more the sounds of joy and gladness, the voices of bride and bridegroom, and the voices of those who bring thank offerings to the house of the LORD, saying, "Give thanks to the LORD Almighty, for the LORD is good; his love endures forever." For I will restore the fortunes of the land as they were before,' says the LORD.

(Jer. 33:10-11)

~ ~ ~

And the man took a breath of air and looked up at blue sky. Birds were in flight and it was early morning. Clouds floated loose above the world, changing shapes and drifting free. They were as white as newborn lambs. Adam watched some of them release crystal clear water over the earth below, and his eyes followed the drops entering the mist now lifting from the glory of God's creation.

It was rugged, it was beautiful, and it was filled with freedom and easy movement. It was peaceful. It was good—"very good." With the mist now fading into the early part of the day, Adam rose and walked among the trees being fed by streams and rivers. Springs of crystal clear water bubbled up through grasses and other plants growing on the land. He could hear the sounds of life and feel the pleasure of being alive.

As he enjoyed his walk, God talked to him about the birds that flew overhead and the animals living everywhere. God brought each of them to Adam to see what he would name them, knowing it was not good for Adam to be alone. But Adam would not find a suitable companion and helper among the animals.

"So the Lord God caused Adam to fall into a deep sleep; and while he was sleeping, he took one of his ribs and closed up the place with flesh." Then God made a helper for Adam out of his rib and brought her to him.

When he opened his eyes, he saw her. He named her "woman," because she was taken out of him—the first man. Adam also said, "This is now bone of my bones and flesh of my flesh."

Adam and Eve knew nothing of good or evil. Everything was perfect—their thoughts, their conversations, their actions—all perfectly united as if they were one being. They enjoyed each other's company and all God wanted for them in their relationship. Since shame was not present in any form, they did not experience it.

(from Gen. 1-2)

The world is different today and men have fallen from the intimacy of their beginning. Satan still roams, spreading his lies and working to bring the world to a desolate waste, without men or animals. He wants to confuse and to distort the purpose of a man's relationship with a woman. He wants to fill their hearts with shame.

Yet, the sounds of joy and gladness have entered the land again through the birth of the Lord God's son—Jesus.

The voices of the bride and bridegroom lift into the air. Their laughter sounds in joyous concert. They walk into the house of the Lord together and give Him thanks for His goodness. He restores their lives and their intimacy so that they are once again without shame.

REBUILDING INTIMACY—PART II
(your thoughts and actions)

Describe an intimate relationship apart from a sexual interaction.

_____

_____

_____

_____

_____

_____

What separates you from having an intimate relationship? Is it in the present or the past? Is it a particular sin that you are engaged in at present, that you know is wrong and yet you rationalize its existence anyway? Ask God to heal you or take it from you.

_____

_____

_____

_____

_____

_____

Describe your relationship with your biological father. Is it an intimate one?

_____

_____

_____

_____

_____

Who has taught you the most about what an intimate life looks like, and what has that person taught you?

_____

_____

_____

_____

_____

_____

While you may be single and unmarried, I want you to understand that the relationship between a man and a woman requires much work, sacrifice, and dependence upon God. As time passes, this work pays off in a stronger and closer union with your bride—one that approaches the life God envisioned for you both.

Men Soar Like Eagles!

DO YOU NOT know? Have you not heard? Has it not been told you from the beginning? Have you not understood since the earth was founded? He sits enthroned above the circle of the earth, and its people are like grasshoppers. He stretches out the heavens like a canopy, and spreads them out like a tent to live in. He brings princes to naught and reduces the rulers of this world to nothing.

No sooner are they planted, no sooner are they sown, no sooner do they take root in the ground, than he blows on them and they wither, and a whirlwind sweeps them away like chaff.

"To whom will you compare me? Or who is my equal?" says the Holy One. Lift your eyes and look to the heavens: Who created all these? He who brings out the starry host one by one, and calls them each by name. Because of his great power and mighty strength, not one of them is missing.

Do you not know? Have you not heard? The LORD is the everlasting God, the Creator of the ends of the earth.

He will not grow tired or weary, and his understanding no one can fathom.

He gives strength to the weary and increases the power of the weak.

Even youths grow tired and weary, and young men stumble and fall; but those who hope in the LORD will renew their strength. They will soar on wings like eagles; they will run and not grow weary, they will walk and not be faint.

(Isa. 40:21-31)

Have you ever owned chickens? We purchased three a few months ago along with a coop. Since then, we've learned how to feed and water them, predator proof the coop, and trap raccoons looking for an evening meal.

We have one left, and now we've put up pie plates on wires stretched across a garden next to the coop. We've done this to keep hawks away from where we let them out to forage for food. We're not sure which predator got the last one, but we think it was the flying kind.

Early in grade school, we called each other, "Chicken!" And now, after tending to them for a few months, I know why. It's doesn't matter whether it's day or night, something threatens these feathered creatures, so they are always looking around for danger.

Some are braver than others. They get eaten first.

You and I can leave our fear and step out into the light or the darkness with hope. We can look at the heavens and know that our Father created them. As David explains:

"O Lord, our Lord, how majestic is your name in all the earth! You have set your glory above the heavens. From the lips of children and infants you have ordained praise because of your enemies, to silence the foe and the avenger. When I consider your heavens, the work of your fingers, the moon and the stars, which you have set in place, what is man that you are mindful of him, the son of man that you care for him? You made him a little lower than the heavenly beings and crowned him with glory and honor.

You made him ruler over the works of your hands; you put everything under his feet: all flocks and herds, and the beasts of the field, the birds of the air, and the fish of the sea, all that swim the paths of the seas.

O LORD, our Lord, how majestic is your name in all the earth!"

(Psalm 8)

— —

The Holy God of the uerse will not grow wearing tending to you. You will receive His strength for the work of your hands today and for what lies ahead tomorrow. When you grow tired and weariness comes upon you, He will uplift you and bring you power, and when you stumble and fall He will catch you and help you stand.

— —

MEN SOAR LIKE EAGLES
(your thoughts and actions)

What about it—chicken or eagle? How often does your concern turn to control and then to anger?

_____

_____

_____

_____

_____

Read the previous verses from Isaiah again. What part of this passage speaks directly to your heart?

_____

_____

_____

_____

_____

It's not that we must always change the circumstances to find peace or hope: it's that we must remember a truth that is faintly in the background, that when brought boldly forward encourages our way. What do you need to remember to renew your strength?

_____

_____

_____

_____

_____

We truly can soar like an eagle even in the face of great difficulty—even in the face of death. For that to happen, men of God...

_____

_____

_____

_____

_____

_____

You will walk.
You will run.
You will be crowned with glory and honor as His sons.
You will soar like eagles.

Hallelujah, Praise His Name in all the Earth!

"Be Still and KNOW that I am God."

Psalms 46:10

A Man Moved by God

Be Still and Know That He Is God

I GREW UP in church. I can't remember a time when I didn't go to church. I don't remember a time when I didn't "have Jesus in my life." I don't have a conversion story like you hear a lot of times. You see, I am a preacher's kid, "PK" for short. We were always at church. My life revolved around "church", and because of that I was labeled, "a good Christian young man."

When I became a teenager, I noticed that certain aspects of my life didn't add up. We were a poor family, and my dad preached a lot on money. But I remember as a young child, I would sit in the grocery store buggy, peeling off the price tags, looking for a lower price, just as my mom instructed me. Our extended family seemed to have an unusually large number of "premature births" among the first born. My dad preached about how everyone was equal in God's eyes, but could tell "black jokes" like the best of them. We would drive by fishermen on Sunday mornings saying things like, "those poor men...they could be fishers of men...." My life didn't make sense.

God designed me as a scientist. I know this now. I asked questions about everything. Unfortunately, my parents could not answer all my questions. When they did, the answers were something to the effect of, "because God did it...." This led to unspoken frustration, but I didn't stop going church. I stayed "a good Christian young man."

College is where my questions were finally answered, and my faith initially tested. Science explained how the uerse was made! Mathematics did not contradict! Physics proved how the world worked! And I never heard, "because God did it." The answers made sense. And just what I needed to ultimately question my faith: I failed Religion 101. A *"preacher's kid who knows everything about the Bible, never missed a Sunday,"* FAILED religion! But I still "went" to church. I was still known as "a good Christian young man." But the whole time I was thinking, "if science can explain how we got here, then why should I continue coming here?" But, I still went.....

After college, I decided to go to graduate school. It was during this time that I was my most cynical of Christianity (even though I continued to go to church). I studied organic chemistry, but deep down, I was trying to prove that God didn't exist. During the day, I would perform experiments in the lab, while at night, researching journal articles on evolution, The Big Bang Theory, or DNA sequencing. I was convinced it was a matter of time before I would come across the "Holy Grail", proving that God didn't exist. All the while, I still went to church.

I had been at the chemistry department for about two years when I discovered that one of the chemistry professors was a Christian. I asked myself, "How is it possible for someone who is a Christian to be a teacher of science?!?" I made up a reason to go see him, fully intending to trap him with my questions. I had been studying science vs. religion for a couple of years now. He needed to be set straight, and I was clearly the one to do it! I went by his office for what I thought would be a quick discussion. I left over an hour later, my mind blown. He completely obliterated my cynicism for Christianity, in a loving, yet firm manner. For every one of my questions, he had a response, and they were not "because God did it." They were simple, calculated answers that did not in any way contradict the teachings of Christianity. But more importantly, it was the way he responded: calmly, peacefully, patiently, and lovingly. It was as if he had been expecting this conversation for some time. You could tell he cared, but he didn't condemn.

One thing he said to me has stuck with me all these years later: "Science and mathematics are nothing more than man's way of explaining God's creation." You cannot begin to appreciate how calming this phrase is to someone who continues to go to church even after they can explain evolution, The Big Bang Theory, how molecules work, or the functionality of DNA. This simple statement was my "light bulb" moment. I am convinced that God placed this professor in my life, at that moment, to nudge me in His direction.

As a scientist who is a follower of Jesus, I look to His creation to better understand how He is interacting with mankind. Today, I use my experience to help others see how science does not contradict Christian beliefs. I do this through formal teaching environments, but more importantly I do this through how I live my life. I try my best to answer my kids' questions about the world they live in by saying things like, "this is HOW God did this. Let me explain...." I spend time with other scientists, discussing theories about our environment; them knowing full well that I am a Christian who is not condemning them.

For me, science says, "this is how God did it." It's my belief that scientists are simply discovering how God made the world. The Big Bang Theory is nothing more than God saying, "Let there be light!" Science does not contradict what God says. It shows how He does it. When we accept that God "does it", and science is <u>the way</u> He does it, our lives can be so much more at peace.

Romans 1:19-20 (ESV) has a very personal meaning to me: *"For what can be known about God is plain to them, because God has shown it to them. For his invisible attributes, namely, his eternal power and divine nature, have been clearly perceived, ever since the creation of the world, in the things that have been made. So they are without excuse."*

God has always been there, and He will always be there (Rev. 1:8). He interacts with us in different ways, not JUST in church on Sundays. We can experience Him through science, music, art, relationships, and even nature! For those of us who struggle with questions while attending church, it's ok to ask questions. Remember: God is always present, even for good Christian young men who don't get all their questions answered.

Ironically, telling my personal story is rather difficult in comparison to my tendency to bloviate and opine. However, the exercise was refreshing, frustrating, anxious, and peaceful. It helped to focus on the key aspects of my story, when God was saying, "that was Me, drawing you to Me."

Men Avoid HER!

MY SON, KEEP my words and store up my commands within you. Keep my commands and you will live; guard my teachings as the apple of your eye. Bind them on your fingers; write them on the tablet of your heart. Say to wisdom, "You are my sister," and call understanding your kinsman; they will keep you from the adulteress, from the wayward wife with her seductive words.

At the window of my house, I looked out through the lattice. I saw among the simple, I noticed among the young men, a youth who lacked judgment. He was going down the street near her corner, walking along in the direction of her house at twilight, as the day was fading, as the dark of night set in.

Then out came a woman to meet him, dressed like a prostitute and with crafty intent. (She is loud and defiant, her feet never stay at home; now in the street, now in the squares, at every corner she lurks.) She took hold of him and kissed him and with a brazen face she said:

"I have fellowship offerings at home; today I fulfilled my vows. So I came out to meet you; I looked for you and have found you! I have covered my bed with colored linens from Egypt. I have perfumed my bed with myrrh, aloes and cinnamon. Come, let's drink deep of love till morning; let's enjoy ourselves with love! My husband is not at home; he has gone on a long journey. He took his purse filled with money and will not be home till full moon."

With persuasive words she led him astray; she seduced him with her smooth talk. All at once he followed her like an ox going to the slaughter, like a deer stepping into a noose till an arrow pierces his liver, like a bird darting into a snare, little knowing it will cost him his life.

Now then, my sons, listen to me; pay attention to what I say. Do not let your heart turn to her ways or stray into her paths. Many are the victims she has brought down; her slain are a mighty throng. Her house is a highway to the grave, leading down to the chambers of death.

(Prov. 7)

The sirens call and men sail their ships through the warm mist onto the waiting rocks. The collision tosses their bodies into the frigid waters. The pain of cold and ice break the warmth and excitement of the moments just before. Their smothered senses awake to reality, but it's too late. Many die. Very few recover to a life without remembrance of that one event. They feel the waves of impact in the years after them. And what about the children left floating in the waters?

Stealing, murder, adultery—What do these have in common? How do these flow together in a wider and deeper ocean of entanglement? When you take another man's wife, what do you steal? What do you kill? How do these three sound together like an angry storm breaking on the shoreline? What is broken in that storm? What do you think when you read, "A man will leave his father and mother and be united to his wife, and they will become one flesh" (Gen. 2:24), or, when you read the words of Jesus, "I tell you that anyone who divorces his wife, except for marital unfaithfulness, causes her to become an adulteress, and anyone who marries the divorced woman commits adultery (Matt. 5:32)?" Trust, oneness, intimacy, shame; and yet, she comes to meet him as the day is fading and as the dark of night sets in. Who is she? For many she is a woman. For others she is riches, or power, or fame. Whatever we call her, her purpose remains the same; with a brazen face she destroys your relationship with God or with your earthly bride.

Men of God desire wisdom. They do not want to face the darkness as a boy. Judgment and discernment, these they pursue. Wisdom guards their thinking and keeps them from what or who may call them into disaster. They steer their lives away from disaster, and the mist cannot overcome the brilliance of their sight. At all cost, they protect the relationship formed between man and woman and between man and God.

The harlots of the night beckon them, but a light leads them away. *In the beginning was the Word, and the Word was with God, and the Word was God. The same was in the beginning with God. All things were made by Him; and without Him was not any thing made that was made. In Him was life; and the life was the light of men* (John 1:1-4 KJV).

For those who have been saved from the wrecks of life and for those who have wrecked their ships and are coming home, there is now no condemnation for those who are in Christ Jesus (Rom. 8:1).

His house will be a house of prayer. His house will be a highway to life. His house will be a fortress for all men. Seek His wisdom for the rest of your days. He will open your eyes and reveal the path away. Walk away, run. Avoid HER! Choose Him!

MEN AVOID HER
(your thoughts and actions)

Which of these has the greatest power of seduction over you? Women, power and control, perfection, significance, or comfort?

_____

_____

_____

_____

_____

_____

When the sirens call and sound out your greatest temptation, what's the promise that never really satisfies, never delivers?

_____

_____

_____

_____

_____

_____

What truth can replace the lie behind the things that tempt you most?

_____

_____

_____

_____

_____

Find some words of God in the Bible that will help you remember what's important and true. Memorize them. Carry them with you.

Please remember, for those who have been saved from the wrecks of life, and for those who have wrecked their ships and are coming home, there is now no condemnation for those who are in Christ Jesus.

Avoid HER! Choose Him!

DAY 30

Men Forgive!

MESSAGES FROM JESUS

Therefore, if you are offering your gift at the altar and there remember that your brother has something against you, leave your gift there in front of the altar. First go and be reconciled to your brother; then come and offer your gift.

So watch yourselves. "If your brother sins, rebuke him, and if he repents, forgive him. If he sins against you seven times in a day, and seven times comes back to you and says, 'I repent,' forgive him.

For if you forgive men when they sin against you, your heavenly Father will also forgive you. But if you do not forgive men their sins, your Father will not forgive your sins.

In anger his master turned him over to the jailers to be tortured, until he should pay back all he owed. "This is how my heavenly Father will treat each of you unless you forgive your brother from your heart."

Bear with each other and forgive whatever grievances you may have against one another. Forgive as the Lord forgave you.

Father, forgive them, for they do not know what they are doing.

(Matt. 5:23-24; Luke 17:3-4; Matt. 6:14-15;
Matt. 18:34-35; Col. 3:13; Luke 23:34)

None of us is perfect. Once I asked a man if he would be interested in joining a group that was gathering to learn and grow as men of God. He said, "I really don't have it all together, know little about God, and don't really know what I would have to offer." I replied, "When you have it all together, don't come, because this group of guys doesn't have it all together either, and never will!"

I grew up in an imperfect family, did you?

When I look back at my life up until now, I can see a ton of personal mistakes. I've traveled in the wrong direction, said things I wish I could take back, and hurt people knowingly and unknowingly. Every church, business, and family has at least one thing in common. They are made up of bumbling, fumbling, grudge-holding people, and they carry their grievances next to their heart. I have been one of those people.

Some men have been hurt in more lasting ways—a child was killed in a car accident or in a drive-by shooting. You may have been slandered, tortured, bullied or ridiculed in public, or rejected by your spouse or fiancé and then discarded for another's affections. Parental abuse for many has caused physical and mental pain. As a result, a single word or behavior can now trigger anger just because of something that occurred years ago, and today you allow the bitterness of the event to keep you in bondage.

I know men who carry the sting of regret over bad decisions, something they didn't do or did do, and the people they hurt. These men cannot forgive themselves.

I know men who carry resentment toward God—blaming Him for what happened to them or for what exists in a world of decay and immorality. Perhaps a child died or a girlfriend was raped or life just didn't turn out like they expected. These men cannot forgive God.

What do we do to find peace and joy? How do men free themselves from the bitterness that rests next to their hearts?

There is not an easy formula, but it starts with looking to the cross and hearing Jesus say, "Father, forgive them, for they do not know what they're doing." (Luke 23:34) He understands your pain. He felt the anguish of mental and physical mistreatment and died in great agony. And though He did not fall to sin, He did experience enormous temptation from the most powerful angel in God's kingdom—Satan: "we do not have a high priest who is unable to sympathize with our weaknesses, but we have one who has been tempted in every way, just as we are, yet was without sin." (Heb. 4:15) "And at the ninth hour Jesus cried out in a loud voice, "Eloi, Eloi, lama sabachthani?"—which means, "My God, my God, why have you forsaken me?" (Mark 15:34)

Pray. Tell Him about what troubles you. Tell Him about your grievances, what you faced and how it felt. Remember His example, His wounds and His suffering for your sins, and then turn and forgive them all, including yourself and, if necessary, forgive God. In the prayers that form, explain the pain of your injuries, your bitterness, your anger and then forgive each of your torturers for what they did, and he will set you free.

Lastly, remember this:"... *our struggle is not against flesh and blood, but against the rulers, against the authorities, against the powers of this dark world and against the spiritual forces of evil in the heavenly realms" (Eph. 6:12)*. That's why Jesus while dying on the cross looked out at the soldiers and those jeering at him and said, *"Father forgive them, they do not know what they are doing"* (Luke 23:34).

We are all blinded by temptation and sin that wrap around our senses as we hurt other people. In the final stages, having lost all sensitivity to the righteousness of God, a person gives themselves over to a life of sensuality. Then, they can no longer hear or see the lack of God in what they do, or they would turn and Jesus would heal them (read Eph. 4:17-19).

"He has blinded their eyes and deadened their hearts, so they can neither see with their eyes, nor understand with their hearts, nor turn—and I would heal them." (John 12:40)

MEN FORGIVE
(your thoughts and actions)

Pray and then make a list of everyone you have not forgiven in your life. Start with your family and your childhood and continue until you reach this moment. If you need to place yourself or God on this list, do so.

_____

_____

_____

_____

_____

Start with the first name on the list and pray Holy Father, _____
_____ (name) _____
(what they did) and it made me feel _____
(tell Him how it affected you). Through your power and with Your grace and mercy, I forgive (him/her) and release myself from all bitterness, anger, and resentment in my heart. (Do this for every name on the list, and if you need to, include yourself, and if necessary, God.)

_____

_____

_____

_____

_____

As you move forward with a new beginning, listen to the Spirit of God and do not allow a need to forgive to remain undone. Use the prayer above as a model, and rid yourself of anger, ill will, or revenge. Forgive them with God's power.

_____

_____

_____

_____

_____

_____

Ask Jesus to power your confession and forgiveness. He will do it with and for you. Do not hold onto your bitterness. Desire freedom from the constant torture. Let go with Him, and if you need help taking something before God, there are men of God ready to help you.

DAY 31

Men Love Children!

ONLY BE CAREFUL, and watch yourselves closely so that you do not forget the things your eyes have seen or let them slip from your heart as long as you live. Teach them to your children and to their children after them.

Hear, O Israel: The LORD our God, the LORD is one. Love the LORD your God with all your heart and with all your soul and with all your strength. These commandments that I give you today are to be upon your hearts. Impress them on your children. Talk about them when you sit at home and when you walk along the road, when you lie down and when you get up.

Jesus said, "Let the little children come to me, and do not hinder them, for the kingdom of heaven belongs to such as these."

People were bringing little children to Jesus to have him touch them, but the disciples rebuked them. When Jesus saw this, he was indignant. He said to them, "Let the little children come to me, and do not hinder them, for the kingdom of God belongs to such as these. I tell you the truth, anyone who will not receive the kingdom of God like a little child will never enter it."

Fathers, do not embitter your children, or they will become
discouraged.

(Deut. 4:9; Deut. 6:4-7; Matt. 19:14; Mark 10: 13-16; Col. 3:21)

A few weeks ago, our grandson, Maxwell, entered the world. When
I held him on my chest facing me, he got fidgety and fretful until
I turned him around. He wanted to see the open room around
him. As I watched, I could see his eyes follow patterns, colors, and
movements with innocent wonder. His arms lifted in cadence to
the people as he responded to their attention.

The best part was when he smiled at me. What a moment.

Are you aware that child trafficking goes on in the world?
Someone told me that if your child is stolen at an amusement
park, her hair and outfit will be changed, and within 30 minutes,
someone will be walking her out the front gate. This actually
happened to some folks in our town and the police were able to
stop the kidnappers and retrieve the child as they were attempting
to leave the park.

Jesus loves children and He left special instructions for men
regarding their treatment. From an early age, we should take an
active part in their spiritual development and love for God. This
means bedtime stories, prayers at dinner and before bed, and open
discussions about our faith and hope. It also means listening and
responding to their questions. It mostly means being a spiritual
role model, someone who follows Jesus and is an ambassador of
His strength, grace, and love.

Jesus also gave us this warning: *"But if anyone causes one of
these little ones who believe in me to sin, it would be better for him
to have a large millstone hung around his neck and to be drowned
in the depths of the sea"* (Matt. 18:6).

We discipline our children with kindness and gentleness, keeping our anger in check (something I was imperfect at doing). As fathers, we do not want to embitter our children. We do not want them discouraged and feeling condemned and unworthy of forgiveness or love. We want them to enter society knowing that Jesus and their parents love them, especially during times of imperfection. We want them able to bounce back and fight against obstacles without fear of losing our love and knowing they are of great value. And most importantly if they wander from Him, rebel, or lose their way, we want them to know that Jesus will always love them, always forgive them, and always come running to them when they want to return.

MEN LOVE CHILDREN
(your thoughts and actions)

Please read John 1:12 and 1 John 3:1 and start with yourself. Know that you are a child of God. Train yourself in godly matters. Through God's power, discipline yourself and take care of your body, your mind, and your heart.

_____

_____

_____

_____

_____

_____

When you make mistakes or sin, don't abhor yourself or live in condemnation. When guilt surfaces, make amends, say you're sorry, confess with a repentant heart, and accept God's grace and forgiveness. Then, work to be different and better in God's power. Move on in freedom.

_____

_____

_____

_____

_____

_____

When children are in your care, teach them about God and about Jesus. Pray with them. Pray around the dinner table and on all kinds of occasions—even those of celebration. Discipline them out of love and make sure they know you love them especially after and during these times. Remember, you are not perfect either and you have a grace-filled Heavenly Father who forgives you and loves you always.

_____

_____

_____

_____

_____

_____

Finally, be an ambassador of Christ and a mentor to children and to young men and women as you age. This is the splendor of having gray and white hair—to be an emissary of the Father to those He brings near. Write down the names of those closest to you now for whom you might be a spiritual sage.

_____

_____

_____

_____

_____

_____

So, love children and love God, and if YOU are far away from Him, come on home. He's waiting and watching for your return—always.

"Yet to all who received him, to those who believed in His name, He gave the right to become children of God...How great is the love the Father has lavished on us, that we should be called children of God!" (John 1:12; 1 John 3:1)

DAY 32

Men Return Home!

THERE WAS A man who had two sons. The younger one said to his father, "Father, give me my share of the estate." So he divided his property between them.

Not long after that, the younger son got together all he had, set off for a distant country, and there squandered his wealth in wild living. After he had spent everything, there was a severe famine in that whole country, and he began to be in need. So he went and hired himself out to a citizen of that country, who sent him to his fields to feed pigs. He longed to fill his stomach with the pods that the pigs were eating, but no one gave him anything.

When he came to his senses, he said, "How many of my father's hired men have food to spare, and here I am starving to death! I will set out and go back to my father and say to him: Father, I have sinned against heaven and against you. I am no longer worthy to be called your son; make me like one of your hired men." So he got up and went to his father.

But while he was still a long way off, his father saw him and was filled with compassion for him; he ran to his son, threw his arms around him and kissed him.

The son said to him, "Father, I have sinned against heaven and against you. I am no longer worthy to be called your son."

But the father said to his servants, "Quick! Bring the best robe and put it on him. Put a ring on his finger and sandals on his feet. Bring the fattened calf and kill it. Let's have a feast and celebrate. For this son of mine was dead and is alive again; he was lost and is found." So they began to celebrate.

Meanwhile, the older son was in the field. When he came near the house, he heard music and dancing. So he called one of the servants and asked him what was going on. "Your brother has come," he replied, "and your father has killed the fattened calf because he has him back safe and sound."

The older brother became angry and refused to go in. So his father went out and pleaded with him. But he answered his father, "Look! All these years I've been slaving for you and never disobeyed your orders. Yet you never gave me even a young goat so I could celebrate with my friends. But when this son of yours who has squandered your property with prostitutes comes home, you kill the fattened calf for him!"

"My son," the father said, "you are always with me, and everything I have is yours. But we had to celebrate and be glad, because this brother of yours was dead and is alive again; he was lost and is found." (Luke 15:11-32)

Have you ever left a time of peace and safety and entered a new world where the excitement carried you into unhealthy activities? Maybe the new wore off and what was left was a remembrance of a better place somewhere in the past? It's also possible that you left home and life became brighter. It filled with greater joy and peace because of better surroundings and role models of faith.

When men leave home, living becomes better or worse. It's seldom the same.

Do you know what it's like to squander the opportunities or money you've had pass through your hands? Have you handled your relationships with respect? What about the chances you've had to get advice before taking action? Did you look past those possible mentors or did you sit and listen to their wisdom? Have you acted before you got someone to help you think? If so, each step in this life may have carried you further from God's plan for you.

For thousands of years, men have forgotten who they are and who made them. They've wandered far from home and from God. Immersing themselves in the world, they've stopped searching for their roots." With deadened spiritual senses, they've dived further and further into secularism and humanism. God became dead for them.

Is any of this you? Are you hanging on by a thread of faith? Are you sitting in a bunch of trouble that threatens to overcome you? Are you depressed with the grasping and striving that never seems to bring you satisfaction? Do you believe that God cares for you despite the life you've lived?

MEN RETURN HOME
(your thoughts and actions)

Hopefully, if you're this far into this study, and you've been absent from the Father and from His Son, you've already started back home. However, The Barna Group (an evangelical Christian polling firm based in Ventura, California) after 15,000 interviews, found that many Christians do not feel that they have surrendered and submitted fully to God. They've also substituted a broken and contrite heart with faithful activities. It's been a long time since they've been contrite and repentant before God. As a result, they do not experience a profound intimacy with and love for God and a profound compassion for humanity.

Describe your faith walk and relationship with Jesus at this time. Is He present in your life? Do you relate to the Apostle Paul's words, "I have been crucified with Christ and I no longer live, but Christ lives in me and the life I now live I live in the body, I live by faith in the Son of God who loved me and gave Himself up for me" (Gal. 2:20)?

_____

_____

_____

_____

_____

_____

Read Psalm 51. What does God's Spirit reveal to you?

_____

_____

_____

_____

_____

_____

Read Psalm 103. What does God's Spirit reveal to you?

_____

_____

_____

_____

_____

_____

Men of God return home. As they do, they look around to see where God is working—with whom He is working—and they tell them about Jesus. Look around this week with a love for God and a profound compassion for humanity born out of Jesus working in you. Pray for those around you. Share the good news as you experience Him in your life. Now, who is close to you with whom you can share the good news of Jesus?

_____

_____

_____

_____

_____

_____

Here's the promise. Take one step, one beat of your heart moving back in His direction and He'll coming running to you. That's what the parable says. And when He finds you, He will celebrate with music and dancing over your return.

You'll be alive again—not lost, but found!
Return to Him. Take steps in His direction!
Join us in the great adventure and the good news of Jesus Christ!

"There is now no condemnation
for those who are in Christ Jesus,
because through Christ Jesus the
law of the Spirit who gives life
has set me free from the law
of sin and death."

Romans 8:1-2

A Man Moved by God

There Is Now No Condemnation

IN WRITING THIS, I felt like I was cut in two. I pray that whatever appears on this page serves to point back to Him and shine His light on the lies of the deceiver.

This is not a story of heroic comebacks. There are no "against all odds" moments where a brave warrior draws a line in the sand.

This is a story of self-deception, vain gratification, and despair. The hero part happened over 2000 years ago.

My childhood was remarkably unremarkable. Compared to the countless stories I have heard from other men my age, I actually experienced very little pain and personal struggle. My family was intact and supportive; we experienced no financial hardship, and my health was never in question. Academics, athletics, and social skills were all mind numbingly average. The total absence of anything exceptional was perhaps the only exceptional part of my first 14 years on earth. And then I met the deceiver....

At age 14, I transferred by necessity from a utopian tiny private Christian school to a large public high school. As a freshman transfer, I knew exactly two people in the entire school. I still remember the first day of class: the wrong clothes, the wrong hair, the wrong values. Quickly I learned that my Christian upbringing gained me exactly zero street credibility. The deceiver immediately introduced me to a brand new genre of self-loathing: a wretched emotional state fueled entirely by my dependence on others' approval and continuous comparisons of value based on everything but truth.

In the absence of a personal relationship with God, I looked to religion for relief. New sets of rules, standards, and judgment for myself, and others, provided no relief and in fact cemented the same hatred of self as the peer rejections in my secular life. It was the same song, different verse. And so I chose to embrace the lie. The lie was clear and continuously in front of me. My value as a human, my worth on this earth, was a direct product of my ability to perform. I would only be as good as the most pressing comparison, the most recent success, and the trophies sitting on the deceiver's mantle. The meaning of my life would be to win, to consume, and to win again. It is the same lie that is handed to us every day in the cars that we drive, the houses we covet, the women we lust after, and a never ending push towards endless self-indulgence and the illusion of control.

And so I spent the next 10 years perfecting the lie. I wasn't quite big enough to lead the basketball team, wasn't quite smart enough to run the SGA, and so I carved out a home in the schizophrenic pocket of our social hierarchy. Our group moved among the various cliques without committing to any set of values or relationship. We willingly traded character for acceptance and deceived ourselves with claims of "non-conformity" and "acceptance of all." I still remember the first time I saw a t-shirt with the message, "Better to reign in hell than serve in heaven." It was a perfect summary for the life I had chosen.

For years I embraced the deceiver's lie and my self-worth was never assured. Every failure diminished and every success bloated. Nothing could satisfy. Each promotion, each sexual conquest and each material indulgence fed the lie and made it bigger. As the reality sank in that the deceiver's promises of happiness could never satiate, I began to cover the pain with chemicals, work, and continuous distraction. Over time, the fruits of this life turned into ruined relationships and addictions. My best friend of 13 years threw himself off the Gay Street Bridge to stop the same pain I was feeling...

And so I decided to fix myself.

With enough will, with enough drive, with enough discipline, I would resurrect myself. This would require vast amounts of self-knowledge and tools to control the mind, tools that would allow me to decide my own fate. I needed these tools to function as my own God.

Graduate school, sobriety and a singular focus on understanding the human mind were tools I chose to try and stay in control. The deceiver simply put lipstick on the same pig and we were back in business. Over the next handful of years, I prided myself on the discipline and drive that it took to perform in my graduate program. I congratulated myself on the willingness to use my mind to help others who were in pain. Each elaborate complication allowed me to determine the value and content of my life, never submitting to another man or the Creator. Morality was a function of my own values, a nod to supreme comparison of "living a life of service" versus the selfish enterprise of others around me.

And I hated myself.

God continuously speaks to us. So frequently our ears are full of our own self-deception that He must use massive pain to bring us back to Him. At the age of 34, I checked out. The illusions were burning down. I understood the human mind and even how to facilitate change for those in pain, but the act of loving another when you loath your own self is like pouring hot coals into a gaping wound. And so I left the field through which I defined myself and hid in the safety of business and production. Broken with self-inflicted wounds, I built the haze of activity and distraction that men use to avoid painful truths. Every man who has run from truth understands the daily effort to numb and hide from God. They come to us through our work, through our televisions, and through our bartenders. And still God pursues us.

On July 4th, I took my then fiancé to our favorite wing joint for dinner. We had been on the road for over a week and were well past kind conversation. As we turned out of the restaurant for a quarter mile drive home, I tried to tune out the complaints and frustrations from the passenger seat. And then I woke up in the hospital.

The young man who ran into us was being chased by the police. He was high on cocaine, intoxicated, and driving on a suspended license. And he was going 86 in a 30. The Honda Civic he was driving hit my Suburban exactly one inch behind my driver side door. The force of impact was so great that he cut himself and my vehicle in half. It is amazing the perspective that is afforded by missing death by one tenth of a second. Even the deceiver cannot maintain the illusion when we face our own mortality. He cannot prevent the questions of "why am I still here" and "what does my life really mean" from shattering the distance between man and his creator.

And so I woke up. I woke up to the realization that my value as a man has nothing to do with my performance. It is completely unrelated to what I have, what I consume, or the title on my business card. My value as a man was forever cemented by the heroic efforts of a Savior that took all of my lies, my pain, and my hurt, and then left them nailed to a cross so I could experience true meaning—meaning that replaces my fear with certainty, my selfishness with love, and my illusion with the clarity of truth. This is meaning that cannot be earned, cannot be achieved, it can only be accepted and passed to others who do not deserve it.

My life is not perfect. I struggle each day with the same lies that the deceiver hurls at each of us. But there is a qualitative difference to my existence. It is the knowledge that although I am still in battle, the outcome of the war is known. The knowledge that my life has meaning and worth that cannot be diminished and can never be lost. It is the knowing that regardless of the circumstances of my life, I will always have value and be worthy of love.

DAY 33

Transformation—Part I

"NOW THERE WAS a man of the Pharisees named Nicodemus, a member of the Jewish ruling council. He came to Jesus at night and said, "Rabbi, we know you are a teacher who has come from God. For no one could perform the miraculous signs you are doing if God were not with him."

In reply Jesus declared, "I tell you the truth, no one can see the kingdom of God unless he is born again.""

"How can a man be born when he is old?" Nicodemus asked. "Surely he cannot enter a second time into his mother's womb to be born!"

Jesus answered, "I tell you the truth, no one can enter the kingdom of God unless he is born of water and the Spirit. Flesh gives birth to flesh, but the Spirit gives birth to spirit. You should not be surprised at my saying, 'You must be born again.' The wind blows wherever it pleases. You hear its sound, but you cannot tell where it comes from or where it is going. So it is with everyone born of the Spirit."

"How can this be?" Nicodemus asked.

"You are Israel's teacher," said Jesus, "and do you not understand these things?"

(John 3: 1-10)

— — —

When we put helium in a balloon, we expect it to rise. When we put fuel in a car, we expect it to start. When we turn on a faucet, we expect to see water. In these situations and others, we expect to see something happen as a result of acting on a decision based on faith.

When the light turns green, we go and we believe others will stop for a red light. When we skydive with an instructor, we jump believing we'll arrive back to earth safe and unharmed. When we step on a plane, we believe the pilot will get us to our destination. In all of these scenarios, we believe our actions will cause a good result for us. In all of them, there is an object for our faith—the red light, the instructor, the parachute and the pilot.

Think about it. We all put our faith in something or someone throughout the day. How often do we put our faith in God?

Here is a startling statistic: In the same Barna study I mentioned earlier, only 3 percent of self-identified Christians have surrendered control of their lives to God, submitted to His will for their lives, and devoted themselves to loving and serving God and other people.

— — —

Men, like prodigal sons, come to Jesus lost and broken, with an understanding that they need a Savior. They put their trust in Him. They confess their need for His forgiveness. They ask Him to take control of their lives, and they begin to live by faith.

When men are in Christ, a marvelous gift is given. Their previously dead spirits are reborn by the presence of God's Spirit taking residence within them. They are *"a new creation; the old is gone, the new has come!"* (2 Cor. 5:17) From then on, they are led by the Spirit of God who changes them on the inside, and people on the outside see a different person—one who becomes self-disciplined, peaceful and loving.

THE TRANSFORMATION—PART I
(your thoughts and actions)

Are you better because of Jesus? How are you better?

_____

_____

_____

_____

_____

_____

How has the Spirit of God transformed you in the last five years? What would your loved ones say about your transformation?

_____

_____

_____

_____

_____

_____

What is God doing in your life right now? What is He changing about you?

_____

_____

_____

_____

_____

_____

What has God done for you that you could not do for yourself? What is He doing now that you cannot do for yourself? If you have a difficult time answering this, then does that mean you only do what you can do in your own power? Or, do you strive to advance His kingdom with force so that you move into areas of change and action that will require a power greater than your own? In what ways can you tell others about the work of God in your life?

_____

_____

_____

_____

_____

_____

Men of God live a life of love compelled by Christ's love for them. They get better...not perfect, but better, by the power of His Spirit within them. They talk to God. They listen to Him. They read the stories of old and the words of the Holy Bible to add knowledge and understanding as weapons of truth. They strive forward forgetting what is behind and always looking forward as they work for His glory and to please Him the rest of their lives.

The Transformation—Part II

I DO NOT understand what I do. For what I want to do I do not do, but what I hate I do. And if I do what I do not want to do, I agree that the law is good. As it is, it is no longer I myself who do it, but it is sin living in me. I know that nothing good lives in me, that is, in my sinful nature. For I have the desire to do what is good, but I cannot carry it out. For what I do is not the good I want to do; no, the evil I do not want to do–this I keep on doing. Now if I do what I do not want to do, it is no longer I who do it, but it is sin living in me that does it.

So I find this law at work: When I want to do good, evil is right there with me. For in my inner being I delight in God's law; but I see another law at work in the members of my body, waging war against the law of my mind and making me a prisoner of the law of sin at work within my members. What a wretched man I am! Who will rescue me from this body of death? Thanks be to God– through Jesus Christ our Lord! So then, I myself in my mind am a slave to God's law, but in the sinful nature a slave to the law of sin.

Therefore, there is now no condemnation for those who are in Christ Jesus, because through Christ Jesus the law of the Spirit of life set me free from the law of sin and death.

For I am convinced that neither death nor life, neither angels nor demons, neither the present nor the future, nor any powers, neither height nor depth, nor anything else in all creation, will be able to separate us from the love of God that is in Christ Jesus our Lord.

(Rom. 7:15-8:1, 8:38-39)

Ants are interesting. When I was eight or nine years old, I remember someone teaching me to pour water on them for the fun of it. The instant stress and threat to their lives caused them to fight for survival and crawl on top of their buddies. We watched the war break out and rolled around laughing.

While you read this, news reporters write about violence and the threat of violence for the next day's edition. Late last night, policemen in many parts of the country responded to calls about "domestic disturbances." And as you fight through the day, what do you see within you? Peace?

From an early age, habits form. Our brains wire themselves with instant reactions to certain events and words that trigger us into a protective or pleasure-seeking behavior. Some of these are good; others are sinful. Even the genetics our fathers pass along give us a propensity or 'bent' toward sin, behavior that hurts others and ourselves.

The great apostle Paul penned these words about our "sinful natures" before Christ: *"The acts of the sinful nature are obvious: sexual immorality, impurity and debauchery; idolatry and witchcraft; hatred, discord, jealousy, fits of rage, selfish ambition, dissensions, factions and envy; drunkenness, orgies, and the like."* (Gal. 5:19). John Naish (former Health Features Writer for the Times) writes, "Scientists are also learning how the bad effects of men's lifestyle habits, such as their diet, stress levels, weight and smoking, can be transmitted through the genes in their sperm. Just as disturbingly, it seems that men can pass on addictive behaviors and stress-related depression." (read more here: http://tinyurl.com/k4azfmr)

Today, many men, even Christian men, use this genetic bent as a confirming reason for sin saying, "See, that's how I was made."

⁓ ⁓ ⁓

You, however, are men of God. God's Spirit lives in you. In your inner being, you delight in God's laws and order, and you know who will rescue you from the deadening 'bent' within you—Jesus Christ—and His life-giving Spirit. He gives you the power to put off your old self, which belongs to your former manner of life and is corrupted through your deceitful desires, and He gives you the power to be renewed in the spirit of your minds, and to put on a new self, created after the likeness of God.

When the warning bells of your temptation or behavior are sounded within you, God's Spirit will tell you. Listen, pray, and turn away in His power. To strengthen yourself against these things as you grow in Him each day, read and listen to His words of truth. Take captive your thoughts, as Jesus explains, *"For from within, out of the heart of men, proceed evil thoughts, adulteries, fornications, murders, thefts, covetousness, wickedness, deceit, lasciviousness, an evil eye, blasphemy, pride, foolishness"* (Mark 7:21-22).

Associate with men who fight with and for Him. Always be thankful for His salvation. Serve others.

Your temptations are common to those experienced by other men. God is faithful and will not let you be tempted beyond your ability to stand against it. He will provide you the way of escape. Believe in His power which made the uerse and brought Jesus back from the dead.

⁓ ⁓ ⁓

THE TRANSFORMATION—PART II
(your thoughts and actions)

Do you see the habits within you? God will allow you to see what He wants to work on next. If He showed us all our faults at once, I don't think we could bear it. Is He working in you at this time? If so, where?

_____

_____

_____

_____

_____

Do you make any excuses for your ways and manners, especially the ones that get in the way of your Christ-like witness before God and man? What are they?

_____

_____

_____

_____

_____

Have you heard any warning bells lately, any pangs of conscience in your spirit?

_____

_____

_____

_____

How does your faith need to be strengthened for you to live a life of transformation—one that is continually being made better? What do you need to believe about sin or about God for that to happen?

_____

_____

_____

_____

_____

_____

Remember, when you make mistakes, Jesus died for them—all of them. That's good news. Confess, repent, and fight on without condemnation. Go in peace and strive against the forces of evil that all men fight. Rely on Him for the changes in you, and get better today, and every day, until He takes you home. He will give you what you need to do this.

DAY 35

A Man's Confession

WHEN I KEPT silent, my bones wasted away through my groaning all day long. For day and night your hand was heavy upon me; my strength was sapped as in the heat of summer.

Then I acknowledged my sin to you and did not cover up my iniquity. I said, "I will confess my transgressions to the LORD"- and you forgave the guilt of my sin.

I confess my iniquity; I am troubled by my sin. He who conceals his sins does not prosper, but whoever confesses and renounces them finds mercy.

Therefore confess your sins to each other and pray for each other so that you may be healed. The prayer of a righteous man is powerful and effective.

If we claim to be without sin, we deceive ourselves and the truth is not in us. If we confess our sins, he is faithful and just and will forgive us our sins and purify us from all unrighteousness. If we claim we have not sinned, we make him out to be a liar and his word has no place in our lives.

(Psalm 32:3-5; Psalm 38:18; Prov. 28:13; James 5:16; 1 John 1: 8-10)

The typical greeting between two men goes this way, "How ya doing?" Response, "Fine." They then chat about families, sports, hobbies, work or women. Their conversation stays on the top of the mountain where it is open and the air is light and seldom deepens into the dark places of uncertainty and failure.

What troubles you? What troubles God about you?

There was a time in my life when I knew very few men well. A conversation with God occurred only when I needed help. I didn't know Him. I didn't know myself. I was immersed in the flow of what made me feel good, and I didn't grow in Christ.

My relationship with Jesus was a faint beginning long ago. He was far away and I didn't really see Him, even at Christmas. I didn't really feel grateful nor did I live as if I understood what He had done for me. I did live with faith in God. I did believe in Christ. I didn't talk about my sins with anyone, even in prayer to God.

And then it happened. I couldn't hide any longer. The weight of my sins and their disturbance upon myself, my family and others brought me to my knees. I took God and a few friends and went into the dark places of my failure with their prayers and counsel. I opened up. I confessed.

One night at two in the morning I gave my life and everything in it to God. I told Him of my sorrow. I took responsibility for my sin and I asked Him for His forgiveness. This began a journey of confession and repentance with my Lord that while at times difficult, even very difficult, brought me peace and joy and freedom from sin's bondage. This path has also deepened my relationship with Jesus and I know why His birth and resurrection light up the world for men who know them as good news.

Today, there are men I can call or gather with deep in the mountains or by a river to talk with about my challenges or my sins—not to grumble or complain, but to find strength, wisdom and encouragement in their prayers and counsel. I know them and they know me.

A MAN'S CONFESSION
(your thoughts and actions)

What do you struggle with alone? In the last week, what challenges have you faced without God and without the counsel of other godly men?

_____

_____

_____

_____

_____

_____

Please notice what happens when you make important decisions without seeking God and without the advice of godly men.

_____

_____

_____

_____

_____

_____

Do you tell God about your challenges or specific challenges with sin? Do you seek His power and wisdom over these things? If not, why not, and what do you believe about the nature of God?

_____

_____

_____

_____

_____

_____

Do you pray for other men? Do you ask them to pray for you? When was the last time that happened? What keeps you from doing this?

_____

_____

_____

_____

_____

_____

Confess your sins in prayer to God. Be specific. Give them up and surrender them. Renounce them out loud. Jesus has died for them and His mercy and forgiveness last forever. He came to set you free from sin and the bondage of its condemnation, "and you shall be free indeed." (John 8:36 ASV)

"Confess your sins to each other and pray for each other that you may be healed. The prayer of a righteous man is powerful and effective." (James 5:16)

Be honest before God, and your relationship with Him will open up the depths of His goodness and love. There you will find contentment for your soul.

DAY 36

A Man's Idols

YOU SHALL NOT make for yourself an idol in the form of anything in heaven above or on the earth beneath or in the waters below.

They must no longer offer any of their sacrifices to the goat idols to whom they prostitute themselves. This is to be a lasting ordinance for them and for the generations to come.

Do not turn away after useless idols. They can do you no good, nor can they rescue you, because they are useless.

Who may ascend the hill of the LORD? Who may stand in his holy place? He who has clean hands and a pure heart, who does not lift up his soul to an idol or swear by what is false. He will receive blessing from the LORD and vindication from God his Savior. Such is the generation of those who seek him, who seek your face, O God of Jacob.

When you cry out for help, let your collection [of idols] save you! The wind will carry all of them off, a mere breath will blow them away. But the man who makes me his refuge will inherit the land and possess my holy mountain.

This is what the LORD says: "What fault did your fathers find in me, that they strayed so far from me? They followed worthless idols and became worthless themselves."

Those who cling to worthless idols forfeit the grace that could be theirs.

We know also that the Son of God has come and has given us understanding, so that we may know him who is true. And we are in him who is true—even in his Son Jesus Christ. He is the true God and eternal life. ... Dear children, keep yourselves from idols.

(Deut. 5:8, Lev. 17:7, 1 Sam 12:21, Psa. 24:3-6, Isa. 57:13, Jer. 2:5, Jonah 2:8, 1 John 5:20-21)

He arrived at the train station in Knoxville in 1954. There I was, too small to look over the crowd, standing on a platform with my mom. The train was slowing down. The screams of everyone around me were increasing—including those from my mom. The train stopped. The crowd surged. There he was at the window, then at the open door, hanging there with one arm and waving with the other, smiling—Elvis.

In 1991, a year after his recovery from drugs and alcohol, Stephen King wrote the novel, *Needful Things*. The setting for the book was Castle Rock, Maine. An elderly gentleman opened a new shop there. In it, you could find the keepsake of your dreams for a very reasonable price. His only request? Play a small prank of his choosing on someone else in the town. Each keepsake purchased was exactly the thing that the purchasers needed most for fulfillment. Their desires, however, turned into clutching and hoarding, and the town tore itself apart because of a horror of things needed.

What was Stephen King's inspiration for the book? "I guess I was one of the few people in the United States who thought the eighties were really funny. It was a decade in which people

decided, for a while, at least, that greed was good and that hypoc-
risy was simply another tool for getting along. It was the last hurrah
for cigarettes, unsafe sex, and all sorts of drugs. It was the final
corruption of the Love and Peace Generation—The Big Cop-out—
and I thought it was a case of having to laugh. It was either that,
or cry. I was thinking about all this one night while driving home
from a basketball game, and my thoughts centered on Jim and
Tammy Faye Bakker, of the PTL Club. It occurred to me that in
the eighties, everything had come with a price tag, that the decade
quite literally was the sale of the century. The final items up on the
block had been honor, integrity, self-respect, and innocence."

What do you want more than Jesus, more than a relationship with the
Father, more than intimacy with your bride, more than mentoring
your children or more than integrity and righteousness?

From a man's perspective, Solomon had it all, riches, women,
material possessions and the ability and resources to build whatever his heart desired. Yet, here's what he said: "I tried cheering
myself with wine, and embracing folly—my mind still guiding me
with wisdom. I wanted to see what was worthwhile for men to do
under heaven during the few days of their lives.

"I undertook great projects: I built houses for myself and
planted vineyards. I made gardens and parks and planted all kinds
of fruit trees in them. I made reservoirs to water groves of flour-
ishing trees. I bought male and female slaves and had other slaves
who were born in my house. I also owned more herds and flocks
than anyone in Jerusalem before me. I amassed silver and gold for
myself, and the treasure of kings and provinces. I acquired men

and women singers, and a harem as well–the delights of the heart of man. I became greater by far than anyone in Jerusalem before me. In all this my wisdom stayed with me.

I denied myself nothing my eyes desired; I refused my heart no pleasure.

My heart took delight in all my work, and this was the reward for all my labor.

Yet when I surveyed all that my hands had done and what I had toiled to achieve, everything was meaningless, a chasing after the wind; nothing was gained under the sun" (Eccl. 2:3-11) .

When a man of God turns from it all—from the apple, the desire, the knowledge of good and evil, and his needful things—does he then focus on his self-esteem in other ways? No! The Apostle Paul says about himself, "I have been crucified with Christ and I no longer live, but Christ lives in me. The life I live in the body, I live by faith in the Son of God, who loved me and gave himself for me" (Gal. 2:20). Jesus said, "if anyone would come after Me, he must deny himself and take up his cross daily and follow me" (Luke 9:23).

A man of God finds significance, comfort and power, not in useless idols, but in a life lived in faith that God loves him so much that Jesus died for him. Then, he gives himself for the benefit of others and the glory of God. He fights in battles that save those around him. He enjoys the gifts of God's creation with a grateful heart. He loves people. He loves God.

A MAN'S IDOLS
(your thoughts and actions)

What do you trust in more than God? What do you hoard or hold on to with a clutched spirit?

On a scale of 1-10, how important is your reputation? Would you lie to protect it or compete with others for recognition and honor? How selfish are you?

What comforts do you escape into or that you seek to feel better—ones that lead you into bad behaviors, poor health, anger or depression?

Who or what do you attempt to control that leads to an abuse of power and influence? How often do you hurt people or use empty flattery to get them to do what you want them to do? What, if you lost it, would cause you to want to die?

_____

_____

_____

_____

_____

_____

We lift our souls up to the Lord and the Lord alone. We make Him our refuge and trust. We receive the grace that is ours through Him. We have great worth in Him. We have the blessings that He gives us.

The good news—Christ died for us. He's our friend and brother.

He's all we need.

"Who shall separate us from the love of Christ? Shall trouble or hardship or persecution or famine or nakedness or danger or sword?"

Romans 8:35

A Man Moved by God

Who Shall Separate Us from the Love of Christ?

I WAS RAISED in a small Midwest farm town where life seemed simple and safe. Most people never locked their house, and they left car keys dangling in the ignition. There was a strong sense of trust in our little town.

I was the third child of five kids in my family. I spent most of my time playing with the neighbor kids or involved with an organized sport. To be honest, sports really became my life and identity. I was even dating one of the cheerleaders. Being in a small community, everyone went to church, and that was true of my family as well.

Life just seemed good until my dad came home from the doctor's office and informed us kids that our mother had cancer and the doctors thought she had only three weeks to live. That word "cancer" rocked my world and I did not know what to do with it. I had many questions racing through my head; Why God? Why now? Why my mother? I was getting so angry and confused that I started questioning if God even cared or if He was even real or not. What was our purpose in life anyway?

I carried those questions into my college years. It was there, towards the end of my freshmen year, that I met a student who was carrying a Bible along with his other college books. I asked him why he was carrying a Bible and he told me he had a personal relationship with Christ. I had no idea what that meant. He sat down and explained to me how much God loved me and had a plan for my life, but I could not experience that love and plan because of the sins in my life.

And believe me, I knew the sin issues in my life. This student told me that there was nothing I could do to make my sins right before God and that's why Christ came and died for my sins on my behalf. He told me it was not enough to believe in God; I needed to place my faith or trust in who Jesus is and what He did for me on the cross and to invite Jesus into my heart.

I took that first step and asked Jesus into my life that same afternoon. I can honestly say that was the most important decision I had ever made. It was so scary for me to reflect on the fact that even though I believed in God and went to church every weekend, I did not have a relationship with Him until I invited Him into my life. I think it was then that God birthed a passion in me to tell others about this simple truth. It really was an issue of eternal life with God or eternal separation from God.

For the next three years, I plugged into a Christian ministry on campus that helped train me on how to study the Bible and grow in my faith. My passion to serve God grew and after getting my degree I decided to go full time into the ministry.

I was so excited about my new adventure in serving the Lord full time. I just wanted to make a difference in other people's lives. Needless to say I was not ready for what was going to happen next. My family saw many radical changes take place in my life, but instead of being excited that God was changing my life, they were full of fear and confusion—which quickly turned into anger and rejection. My parents told me how ashamed they were of me that

I would throw my college education away to join some religious group and to top it off beg for money to make a living.

There was such a huge disconnect between what God was doing and how my parents perceived it. I spent the next nine years trying to get my parents approval of my Christian work. During that time, all I did and felt built a prison in my heart of deep pain and rejection. I was confused and unfulfilled. My heart was filled with anger, criticism, revenge, lust, envy, controlling spirit, and much more. I felt like a spiritual hypocrite. I was just stuck spiritually and did not know what to do.

I turned to my boss at the time and told him all that was going on inside my heart. To be honest, I thought it was going to be my last day in ministry when I told him the truth. Instead of firing me, he told me about a new ministry called Freedom in Christ that helped him deal with hard issues in his own life. He had me read *Victory over Darkness* and *The Bondage Breaker* by Neil Anderson. Both books helped lay a biblical foundation to resolve the personal and spiritual conflicts in my heart.

Even though I was a missionary, I had no idea of my true identity in Christ. I learned how to submit to the Lord and resist the enemy through confession of my known sins, renouncing the things that I willfully participated in that did not glorify the Lord, and by forgiving from the heart those who have wounded me and forgiving myself. This allowed me to reconcile with the Lord and begin a healthy process to mature in Christ. This has changed my walk with God and has enabled me to walk in my true freedom in Christ. I don't have to strive any longer to please my family or others for my identity.

I have spent the past twenty-two years helping others discover their new identity in Christ and equipping them to walk in their freedom in Christ. It is such a gift to put people in a safe environment with high confidentiality and see them connect with God and His truth in a fresh new way.

DAY 36

A Man's Story

IN THE BEGINNING God created the heavens and the earth.

A man's own folly ruins his life.

Consider it pure joy, my brothers, whenever you face trials of many kinds, because you know that the testing of your faith develops perseverance. Perseverance must finish its work so that you may be mature and complete, not lacking anything.

The righteous man leads a blameless life; blessed are his children after him.

Although a wicked man commits a hundred crimes and still lives a long time, I know that it will go better with God-fearing men, who are reverent before God.

I know, O LORD, that a man's life is not his own; it is not for man to direct his steps.

This is what the LORD says: "Cursed is the one who trusts in man, who depends on flesh for his strength and whose heart turns away from the LORD. He will be like a bush in the wastelands; he will not see prosperity when it comes. He will dwell in the parched places of the desert, in a salt land where no one lives. But blessed is the man who trusts in the LORD, whose confidence is in him.

He will be like a tree planted by the water that sends out its roots by the stream. It does not fear when heat comes; its leaves are always green. It has no worries in a year of drought and never fails to bear fruit."

Then he said to them, "Watch out! Be on your guard against all kinds of greed; a man's life does not consist in the abundance of his possessions."

(Gen 1:1, Prov. 19:3, James 1: 2-4, Prov. 20:7,
Eccl. 8:12, Jer. 17: 5-8, Luke 12:15)

~ ~ ~

The New Testament begins with the genealogy of Jesus Christ, beginning with Abraham. The fathers and grandfathers within His line lied, murdered, supported multiple wives, worshipped idols, made wise decisions, fought for what was right, and loved God. Their lives were a tapestry of contradictions, defeats, and victories.

~ ~ ~

What if you could travel back in time and watch your grandfather's and your father's births and see who gathered around them? What if you could watch their first steps? What if you could listen to their first words? What if you could observe their interaction with family and friends? What if you could see their disappointments, their failures, and their first sins?

Now, fast forward and watch your life unfold and reveal its many decisions and circumstances. Who and what has shaped your values and beliefs and the fabric of your character? How did your parents affect what you thought of yourself and the world around you? How much of your personality and desires were 'bent' from genetic predispositions? Who did you trust? What did you learn to fear? And if you could sum it up in one sentence, what did your life consist of?

Your past has affected your present. Big decisions and defining moments have woven themselves into your story, and they affect how you behave today. They have even affected what you believe is true about yourself and about God.

— — —

Men of God look at their stories to:

- Confess sins, repent, and turn in another direction with God's power
- Find hope in God's mercy and the capacity to forgive others
- Learn and better face life and its challenges and enjoy God in it
- See God's work in their life and enjoy its effect on others

Jesus redeems your life and He breaks every stronghold set up against it. He forgives your sins. He provides you power to change and to grow into His likeness. He enables you to forgive others and to unburden your future from bitterness. He sets you free from your past and yet helps you learn from it. He teaches you to face your trials and testings with perseverance, hope and character. He makes you alive and fills you with the goodness of God.

Do not live in regret and old desires. Live in thankfulness and the blessings of a blameless life.

Do not wish things had been or ought to be different.

Do not keep looking back. Make today full of loving action.

Do not live in bitterness. Forgive and be forgiven by Jesus.

— — —

A MAN'S STORY
(your thoughts and actions)

Exercise: Write your story. Yes, write it down just like the ones you see in this book. Write about where you were and what you were doing before you found Jesus, what happened when you found Him, strayed from Him and found Him again. Write about the victories and joys He has brought into your life.

_____

_____

_____

_____

_____

_____

Exercise: Tell others about your story and listen to theirs. If you have a son or daughter, tell them about your story.

_____

_____

_____

_____

_____

_____

Exercise: Listen to others more than you talk. Ask about their stories. Ask about their spiritual journey. Ask, "How's your spiritual side?" Listen. Learn.

_____
_____
_____
_____
_____
_____

Exercise: Look for those who have had similar struggles to yours. Tell them about how God helped you. The Apostle Paul tells us to "Comfort those in any trouble with the comfort we ourselves have received from God" (1 Cor. 1:4).

_____
_____
_____
_____
_____
_____

It's over! It's finished! He's done it. Lay all your sins and burdens at the cross and walk away with forgiveness and power—free to love God and people. Pray and work and do good! Pray and work and do good! Pray and work and do good!

God says, "We are God's workmanship, created in Christ Jesus to do good works, which God prepared in advance for us to do" (Eph. 2:10). Now go and do them in freedom from sin and its condemnation. Go and do them. Your story continues.

A Man's Design

WHAT IS MAN that you are mindful of him, the son of man that you care for him?

The LORD God formed the man from the dust of the ground and breathed into his nostrils the breath of life, and the man became a living being.

"Let us make man in our image, in our likeness, and let them rule over the fish of the sea and the birds of the air, over the livestock, over all the earth, and over all the creatures that move along the ground." So God created man in his own image, in the image of God he created him;

Now the LORD God had planted a garden in the east, in Eden; and there he put the man he had formed. The LORD God took the man and put him in the Garden of Eden to work it and take care of it.

Lazy hands make a man poor, but diligent hands bring wealth. Laziness brings on deep sleep, and the shiftless man goes hungry.

A man can do nothing better than to eat and drink and find satisfaction in his work. This too, I see, is from the hand of God. ...

To Adam he said, "Because you listened to your wife and ate from the tree about which I commanded you, 'You must not eat of it,' Cursed is the ground because of you; through painful toil you will eat of it all the days of your life. It will produce thorns and thistles for you, and you will eat the plants of the field. By the sweat of your brow you will eat your food until you return to the ground, since from it you were taken; for dust you are and to dust you will return."

In the spring, at the time when kings go off to war, David sent Joab out with the king's men and the whole Israelite army. They destroyed the Ammonites and besieged Rabbah. But David remained in Jerusalem.

One evening David got up from his bed and walked around on the roof of the palace. From the roof he saw a woman bathing. The woman was very beautiful, and David sent someone to find out about her.

As iron sharpens iron, so one man sharpens another.

Though one may be overpowered, two can defend themselves. A cord of three strands is not quickly broken.

For the husband is the head of the wife as Christ is the head of the church, his body, of which he is the Savior.

Husbands, love your wives, just as Christ loved the church and gave himself up for her ...

In this same way, husbands ought to love their wives as their own bodies. He who loves his wife loves himself. However, each one of you also must love his wife as he loves himself …

— — —

When I was a child, I talked like a child, I thought like a child, I reasoned like a child. When I became a man, I put childish ways behind me.

The glory of young men is their strength, gray hair the splendor of the old.

From the days of John the Baptist until now, the kingdom of heaven has been forcefully advancing, and forceful men lay hold of it.

(Psa. 8:4; Gen. 2:7-8, 2:15; 1:26-27; Prov. 10:4, 19:15, 27:17; Gen. Ecc. 2:24; Gen 3:17-19; 2 Sam. 11:1-3; Prov. 27:7; Ecc. 4:12; Eph. 5:23, 25, 28; 1 Cor. 13: 11; Prov. 20:29; Matt. 11:12)

— — —

What is manhood? How would you explain it to a boy? When does the transition occur? When does a boy put his childhood ways behind him and become a man?

LATE MATURATION

The old manhood markers were:

- § Left home, Got a job, Married a woman, Had kids, Protected the family, Protected the country

Looking at these and considering the sacrifices of the American pioneers and the "Greatest Generation," a few of the outward signs that reflected the man inside were:

§ Courage, Commitment, Responsibility, Leadership, Faithfulness, Work

At what age do we see most of these "markers" take place today? Two hundred years ago, they occurred between 16-19 years of age; then, with societal and schooling changes, age 21 and now, ages 28-32. If the old markers are signs of boys transitioning to men, then boys are remaining boys until their 30s, as Michael Kimmel discusses in his book *Guyland*.

LACK OF MALE MENTORS

1. The industrial revolution brought men off the farms and America experienced a major shift in family life and in men's relationships with their sons. Hours spent hunting and farming and solving problems together created a natural and early mentoring relationship between the man and the boy. These manhood lessons ended as absent fathers began to work long hours away from home.

2. Sara McLanahan, in the MacArthur Research Network, reports, "Whereas in the early 1960s, nearly 90 percent of all children lived with both of their biological parents until they reached adulthood, today less than half of children grow up with both natural parents. Nearly a third are born to unmarried parents, the majority of whom never live together, and another third are born to married parents who divorce before their child reaches adulthood. To further complicate matters, a substantial number of children are exposed to multiple marital disruptions and multiple father figures." And David Popenoe writes in his book *Life without Father*, "In just three decades, between 1960 and 1990, the percentage of children living apart from their biological fathers more than doubled, from 17 percent to 36 percent.

By the turn of the century, nearly 50 percent of American children may be going to sleep each evening without being able to say good night to their dads."

3. Men remain boys, never really growing up, and eventually leave their families and their wives. At the same time, American television and movies continue to replace the masculine heroes of <u>Patriot,</u> <u>Gladiator,</u> and <u>Last of the Mohicans,</u> with female action figures who run police stations, lead powerful raids on enemies, and work around men with slower minds and bodies. We can see this trend in Broadway plays as well.

THE CONSEQUENCES

When men do not behave as men, they get into trouble. Late maturation delays earning power, increases promiscuity, and creates a need to divert their natural aggression (testosterone) somewhere. Where do they go for this release? Often, to women, the Internet, games, sports, gangs, drugs and alcohol.

Here's what the research says about boys growing up without a father.

"85 percent of all children that exhibit behavioral disorders come from fatherless homes" (United States Center for Disease Control).

"Children from low-income, two-parent families outperform students from high-income, single-parent homes. Almost twice as many high achievers come from two-parent homes as one-parent homes (*One-Parent Families and Their Children,* Charles F. Kettering Foundation, 1990).

Add this Barna Group research to the picture: "Young adults rarely possess a biblical worldview ...1/2 of 1 percent aged 19-23 possess this (a biblical) worldview."

Reread the Bible verses at the beginning of this message. If you separate out the mistakes and the warnings, what do you see? Where was a man born? What did he do? What was his relationship with God like? Why was a woman made? If the man had remembered who he was and who God was, how would that have changed his reaction to their temptation?

How does a man of God approach his work and the difficulties associated with it as a result of the fall? How does he treat a woman before and during a marriage? What would he do as God's son?

What is a man's most important function in life? How does this change as he nears his final days on earth?

1. **Men of God love God.** They talk with Him every day because they remember that He made them and cares for them. When they waver in this, they think about Jesus.

2. **Men love and LEAD the world back to God** with the talents He gives them. They stand in the gap between right and wrong. They face their fears, act with courage, accept responsibility and avoid passivity—especially about spiritual matters. They express their hope in God to those around them with words and service. They lead their families into a relationship with Jesus. They treat their brides in the same sacrificial way Christ loved and sacrificed Himself for His church. They forcefully advance the kingdom of God (the rule of God in the heart). They do this with kindness, gentleness, and respect—especially with children.

3. **Men work.** With great diligence, and against obstacles, they hunt and farm for food all the days of their life. They do this as to the Lord and not to men.

4. **Men lean on God's grace and mercy when they fail.** They confess their sins. They repent. They move on in worship with greater wisdom and without condemnation. Their selfishness decreases. Their joy increases.

5. **Men put away childish things.** They put their efforts to things that last and that have eternal significance. They study, apply and grow in wisdom and in their understanding of God and His desires for them. As they mature, they grow in favor with God and with those around them. They live out the roles of warrior, lover, and friend. They look for men of God to mentor them. They listen to their advice and later return the favor to boys and men behind them.

A MAN'S DESIGN
(your thoughts and actions)

Do you love God? On a scale of 1-10, rate your relationship with His Son Jesus. What would happen if you loved God, His Spirit, and His Son more?

_____

_____

_____

_____

_____

_____

In what part of your life will you strengthen your spiritual leadership— family, work, or friendships? How will you approach it? What will be different about your approach and how will that impact you and others?

_____

_____

_____

_____

_____

_____

Stop right now and tell God about your sorrow over past failures. Ask for His forgiveness. Ask for Him to move you to be a better man.

_____

_____

_____

_____

_____

_____

What good things in your life will you now approach in moderation, or put away because they are childish? How will that affect how you use time? How will that impact you and others?

_____

_____

_____

_____

_____

_____

After reading the Bible and living with and without faith in God, I believe as many others do. We are part of a grand adventure that follows a story outline we all love to see in the movies. There is an enemy, and he has been hurt by our hero. Battles still occur every day. People need saving, but because of our hero, victory is assured.

We win! Now be encouraged to be a man of God.

DAY 39

Love and Respect

HUSBANDS, LOVE YOUR wives, just as Christ loved the church and gave himself up for her to make her holy, cleansing her by the washing with water through the word, and to present her to himself as a radiant church, without stain or wrinkle or any other blemish, but holy and blameless. In this same way, husbands ought to love their wives as their own bodies. He who loves his wife loves himself. After all, no one ever hated his own body, but he feeds and cares for it, just as Christ does the church- for we are members of his body.

For this reason a man will leave his father and mother and be united to his wife, and the two will become one flesh. This is a profound mystery-but I am talking about Christ and the church. However, each one of you also must love his wife as he loves himself, and the wife must respect her husband.

He must manage his own family well and see that his children obey him with proper respect.

Fathers, do not exasperate your children; instead, bring them up in the training and instruction of the Lord...

Fathers, do not embitter your children, or they will become discouraged.

Teach the older men to be temperate, worthy of respect, self-controlled, and sound in faith, in love and in endurance.

(Eph. 5:25-33; 1 Tim. 3:4; Eph. 6:4; Col. 3:21; Titus 2:2)

Have you ever lost something that you loved? Perhaps you misplaced it, drove off after laying it on top of your car, or it just disappeared and you miss it. I'm the absent-minded guy. My bride has watched me look for things all my life. I'm a little better now, but it still happens—misplaced keys, hat, coat, etc.

In the first years of our marriage, I lost a bag—a very important sack of rocks. Actually, it contained arrowheads that I had found after hours of searching the riverbanks. Hundreds even thousands of years old, I enjoyed hunting for them like my father had taught me—head down, turning over suspect rocks, keeping focused. It was a hobby that got me outdoors, exercised my patience, rewarded my efforts, and gave me something to brag about to my dad and my brother.

I remember finding the lost bag and opening it to see the chipped edges and points of Native American handiwork. I had found them and I felt the excitement of showing them again. Since I was in the basement of the house we had rented, I ran outside and up the back stairs and into the kitchen where my bride was cooking dinner. I burst through the door, looked her in the eyes, and said, "I'm so glad I found..." well, she thought I was going to say "you," but I said "my arrowheads."

I watched the smile on her beautiful face fade into disappointment. I knew that from that moment on until God took me home I would never be able to say the words, "I'm so glad I found you," and have her receive them well.

With the example of Christ before us, we lead people in a kind and considerate manner—with strength but without anger, with truth but without a harsh and disrespectful tone. When we look at our wives, we see Christ sacrificing himself on a cross while enduring humiliation and pain. We see His example of love. In the same power, we learn to sacrifice a self-focus to love our wives. We work to rebuild lost intimacy into oneness.

Our brides do not have to earn our love. They do not have to be respectful to receive our patience and understanding. They do not have to live up to our "wife checklist" to get our appreciation or approval. We love them because Christ always loves us.

In business, however, we may not be able to keep someone in our company and remain profitable or true to our principles. If we reach that point, we work to part with them, if possible, in a way that allows them to keep their dignity.

While this isn't easy for many of us, it is possible if we walk with Christ, if we remember Him, if we start our days in gratefulness, if we lean on Him, if we approach people with His humility.

Remembering Christ died so that we might live forgiven changes how we approach every conflict. Think about this. If you remember, will you be harsh? If you remember, will you be silent? If you remember, will you be unkind? If you remember, will you hang onto bitterness, or will you forgive?

When in conflict, a man feels disrespected by a woman and a woman feels unloved by a man (read about the biblical and scientific foundation for this in Dr. Emerson Eggerich's book, *Love and Respect*. See also: http//www.loveandrespect.com). This begins a vicious cycle. The man feels disrespected so he reacts without love. The woman feels unloved so she reacts without respect. The man senses disrespect and elevates the lack of love. The woman... and so on, and so on...until one of them leaves without respect and without love.

It does not matter what the woman does, it's our responsibility as men of God to STOP THE CYCLE. Look at Jesus. See Him in your wife. STOP THE CYCLE.

For most of us, this isn't natural. We're either passive when we should be bold, or we're harsh when we should be gentle. However, the power of God gives us the supernatural ability to stop the cycle and allows us to love our brides in a sacrificial way.

LOVE AND RESPECT
(your thoughts and actions)

Does your wife have to meet a checklist of your demands before you will love her? Remember it's not natural for you to give her unconditional love. What can you do each day to show her you love her without looking for her to reciprocate?

_____

_____

_____

_____

_____

_____

See Gary Chapman's *The Five Love Languages* (also http://www.5love languages.com). Do you know what love looks like from the perspective of your bride? Does she want quality time with you, gifts that express your love, physical touch, acts of service, or words of affirmation?

_____

_____

_____

_____

_____

_____

In what ways can you show more respect at work? What can you do to show more respect to the imperfect men who lead you? How can you change how you discuss the failures of leadership? How can you change how you handle the failures of others—those you work with, children and yourself? How can you address problems and yet allow others to keep their dignity? Remember, there are few evil people around you— just imperfect ones.

_____

_____

_____

_____

_____

_____

Now, how can you treat yourself with greater respect? What about the stewardship of your body and the resources God has given you? There is a tie between discipline and love. If you discipline yourself or if God disciplines you, it is a sign of love. Please read Hebrews 12:1-12. Write down what you learn.

_____

_____

_____

_____

_____

_____

1. *Speak up. Do not remain silent. Address issues as they occur. Do not wait. Be bold. Be courageous.*

2. *See that your children obey you, but do not embitter them or discourage them. Let them know you love them and that you have confidence in them after every time of discipline.*

3. *Allow your "self" to be controlled by God. Restrain yourself. In most situations in the world, remain disciplined and gentle. Pray before every crucial conversation and during one if it catches you by surprise. Asking God to guide you always leads to better outcomes.*

4. *When we face evil, true evil, we remove those who harbor it. We remove them from our presence. We do this to protect those that remain.*

A Man's Revelation

THE MAN WITHOUT the Spirit does not accept the things that come from the Spirit of God, for they are foolishness to him, and he cannot understand them, because they are spiritually discerned.

As Jesus was sitting on the Mount of Olives, the disciples came to him privately. "Tell us," they said, "when will this happen, and what will be the sign of your coming and of the end of the age?"

Jesus answered: "Watch out that no one deceives you. For many will come in my name, claiming, 'I am the Christ,' and will deceive many. You will hear of wars and rumors of wars, but see to it that you are not alarmed. Such things must happen, but the end is still to come. Nation will rise against nation, and kingdom against kingdom. There will be famines and earthquakes in various places. All these are the beginning of birth pains. Then you will be handed over to be persecuted and put to death, and you will be hated by all nations because of me. At that time many will turn away from the faith and will betray and hate each other, and many false prophets will appear and deceive many people. Because of the increase of wickedness, the love of most will grow cold, but he who stands firm to the end will be saved. And this gospel of the kingdom will be preached in the whole world as a testimony to all nations, and then the end will come."

— — —

The revelation of Jesus Christ, which God gave him to show his servants what must soon take place. He made it known by sending his angel to his servant John, who testifies to everything he saw—that is, the word of God and the testimony of Jesus Christ. Blessed is the one who reads the words of this prophecy, and blessed are those who hear it and take to heart what is written in it, because the time is near.

"Behold, I am coming soon! Blessed is he who keeps the words of the prophecy in this book."

He who testifies to these things says, "Yes, I am coming soon." Amen. Come, Lord Jesus.

The grace of the Lord Jesus be with God's people. Amen.

(1 Cor. 2:14; Matt. 24:3-14; Rev. 1:1-3, 22:7, 20-21)

— — —

It's the last act of our life. A final setting has been revealed in part by words of metaphor—its curtain still drawn, waiting for the hero to enter one last time.

On the main stage, worldwide action has continued to escalate along multiple battle lines between two forces. Many have made a decision to join one side or the other. They endure the struggles of an epic adventure centuries old.

Those sitting in the audience try to avoid entanglement but find that the two forces fight over them! They hurt from the aftermath of the drama in which they also take part and witness. Others hide under their seats only to find they can still hear and feel the troubles of the battles. A few, their hearts moved, stand, confess, repent, and ask the author to place them in their supporting roles to His Son. Their rebirth and submission to the Son saves them and rescues those near death who follow their example.

From the stage, we hear of "wars and rumors of wars." Some of these play out in the businesses along the streets and even in the homes. There are "famines and earthquakes," as the unnatural becomes the norm. Words of truth begin to disappear as "the love of most grows cold." A winter of deadness begins to smother the land with misery and simple people live in caves of loneliness, despair and fear.

—   —   —

Yet, a light shines in the darkness—its warmth and peace surpasses all understanding. Come, Lord Jesus.

The Spirit of God remains in the hearts of men left behind until the hero returns. Come, Lord Jesus!

With courage and power, they rise up as a band of brothers to fight within the strength of His light. Come, Lord Jesus!

They tear down idols! Come, Lord Jesus!

They rebuild years of lost intimacy with their brides and with God. Come, Lord Jesus!

They soar like eagles. Come, Lord Jesus!

They love God. Come, Lord Jesus!

They love their neighbors and lead them to Him. Come, Lord Jesus!

They lean on His grace and mercy. Come, Lord Jesus!

Then the final curtain is drawn, Jesus returns, and a new earth is revealed, and the sons and daughters of God live with Him blessed ever after. "Now the dwelling of God is with men, and He will live with them. They will be his people, and God himself will be with them and be their God. He will wipe every tear from their eyes. There will be no more death or mourning or crying or pain, for the old order of things has passed away."

This will happen. The Author has written the words into the Book of Life. "He who was seated on the throne said, "I am making everything new!" Then He said, "Write this down, for these words are trustworthy and true" (Rev. 21:5).

A MAN'S REVELATION
(your thoughts and actions)

How do you want your family and the people you know to remember you when the curtain closes for you on this earth?

_____

_____

_____

_____

_____

Are you ready to come out of the audience and join the action on main stage? What roles does God want you to play in it—father, grandfather, son, coach, laborer, or encourager?

_____

_____

_____

_____

_____

What's your identity? Who are you? Write this down now that you've completed this study. You are more than your name. God has given you a position and an identity. What is it?

_____

_____

_____

_____

_____

What is your purpose in life? Complete this sentence, "I am _____
_____ (your identity), and in the great spiri-
tual adventure that we fight everyday, I help my family and the people
around me to: _____
_____ so that they might be _____
_____, and live _____
_____. I have given you some blanks to fill in, but after you
pray to God change any of this to meet what He wants you to write.

*... as it is written: "No eye has seen, no ear has heard, no mind has
conceived what God has prepared for those who love him"– but God
has revealed it to us by his Spirit. The Spirit searches all things,
even the deep things of God. (1 Cor. 2:9, 10)*

You Have What It Takes!

JESUS...

"The Spirit of the Lord will come upon you in power ... and you will be changed into a different person."

1 Sam. 10:6

A Man Moved by God

The Spirit Changes a Man

FROM THE PERSPECTIVE of most onlookers, it appeared that I had finished my childhood school days in Michigan with flying colors and was well on my way to succeeding at whatever I chose to do. I was, after all, a gifted athlete on my way to run track for the Uersity of Tennessee. I had gotten good grades in school with little effort, I was raised in the Catholic church, I had a girl friend, and I was confident that I could do just about anything that I set my mind to. Little did I or anyone else know what kind of baggage I was carrying with me when I set out for Knoxville in 1980.

The truth about who I was back then wasn't revealed to me until my heart was changed some 28 years later by the hand of God. I grew up in a family riddled with alcohol abuse and with friends who condoned drugs, porn, gambling, and more. I now look back at a stellar running career at UT and wonder how I did it and also wonder how much better I could have done if I had Him with me then to keep me focused on what was really important.

I met my beautiful bride Pam in college and we proceeded on a fun but reckless journey together. Eventually I was challenged with some slight injuries when I was in my early 30s and then turned to the bottle and all those other things that would make me feel better, at least for a while. That made any attempt at running seriously again impossible. The struggle with my identity went on for years. I was never happy about my work or my health, and it was taking its toll on my marriage, which eventually produced two children. The baggage that I had let consume me was now being shared with my whole family. That included my family in Michigan. In a drunken brawl, I broke my brother's jaw. That left a scar on the relationship with my family that is still in the healing process.

The victims of alcohol abuse in my family are highlighted by my father, whose drinking and smoking led him to a diminished quality of life before it finally killed him. My sister Denise became another victim at the age of 52. Both of these deaths occurred after He saved me, or I don't know how I could have handled them.

Shortly before we had children, Pam began to feel God calling her and she turned her life over to Christ. I make that sound easy. I guess that is because there are those who fight it for years or maybe most of their years before they get it. That was me. I tagged along to church on occasion and even served in the children's ministry at church out of obligation. But, I was a whitewashed wall however, who even tried to convince Pam that God really didn't exist. She would tell you that I can argue like a lawyer, but no matter how perfect my case was presented, she never caved. That was my first encounter with true faith. I never could understand about the faith that she possessed, until the scales fell from my eyes one day.

That day didn't come for many years, well after Pam started her journey. The drinking became worse over those years, but eventually I believe that I started to hear God calling me. I was going to church regularly and even went to a small group with Pam. I guess I thought at some point along the way that I had become saved.

I began to ask God to take the drinking from my life, but I was trapped just like my sister was. While I was writing this story it occurred to me that my prayer was flawed. The first thing I needed to pray for was for God to take my heart, and the addictions could then be dealt with. My marriage was, well, *my* marriage and not *ours*. And my life was not His.

One evening after several cold beers, Pam and I got into a bad fight. Push came to shove which lead to police and other family being summoned. Nobody was physically hurt, but Pam took the kids and left that night. I was angry and there was no remorse. I spent three days plotting revenge for what SHE had done. Pam was done. She had spent years trying to change me, which included prayer, but her prayer was different that day. Her prayer to God that day was that she was done trying to change me and that she was putting her trust in God alone to do what He wanted. Then it happened. In the midst of anger and frustration, in the blink of an eye, I was changed forever. I can't explain exactly what happened, and I am sure that is exactly the way He wanted it, but I was suddenly broken. Pam would tell you something indescribable happened in that moment. I can without a doubt say that was the very second that God took my heart.

There was a lot of praying and apologizing to many people that occurred immediately afterwards. There was an immediate impact on my life in several ways. The first thing God did was to renew my discipline and strength to take care of His dwelling place. I began a workout regimen that I thought was no longer possible. I realized that if my reason for wanting to be physically fit was to first glorify Him then it was sustainable. In my previous life the reasons were to look better, to feel better, to be able to hang with my kids, etc. Those types of motivation had always failed me. Another way that He blessed me was with the ability to not sleep in, which might seem like a curse to some. A few months after I was saved there was a kid's camp that I went on with church to help chaperone.

The morning after the camp, I was up at 5:00 am with a desire to open the Word. That blessing has not changed since that day over six years ago. I guess you must be wondering about my struggle with drinking. Well, God did conquer that addiction for me. I did drink a few times after I came to Christ. I decided I could try and keep it away from my family but eventually realized that I didn't want it any more. It was a miracle that I also prayed for my sister. His plan was different for that situation and I struggled for a while to know the answer why. God did send two angels in the form of local utility workers to answer me, but that is another story. He also gave me a message to share at her funeral.

I still serve in the children's ministry at church, but the obligation to serve has now become a desire to be a part of the disciple making work that Jesus has given all His followers. That disciple making begins right in our home with our two kids who can bear witness to what He has done in my life.

There are lots of stories I could share about how great God is—like the one that ends up with my daughter and me getting baptized in the Clinch River in the winter. He has made me joyful, thankful and content in the work that He has given me. Pam and I are in a much better place, and I believe His blessing rests on us. He has made it clear to us how much He loves our union with Him. God continues to unpack that old baggage of mine, and the garments that He removes are pieces of my life that are now used for His glory. His precious blood has cleansed them, and when they are shared with others, they become useful in His kingdom.

"Come into my life. Make me brighter and more beautiful. Make me like you! Make me free!

2 Corinthians 3:17-18

A Man Moved by God

Father, Open My Eyes—Make Me Like You, Make Me Free!

FATHER, OPEN MY EYES

Father, open my eyes. When my eyes are open, obedience to you is not enough. I want to be passionate about you.

When my eyes are opened, my prayer to you will not focus only on you filling my needs. I will talk to you as a friend and lover.

When my eyes are opened, I'll truly believe, "All these things will be added to me, when I seek you first".

When my eyes are opened, your spirit can shape my worries into prayers and petitions to you. You will come and settle me down.

When my eyes are opened, my flesh will not control me, your spirit will fill me up and lead me.

When my eyes are opened, my relationship with you will be more important than a prestigious career.

When my eyes are opened, time with my children will become more important than time management in my career.

When my eyes are opened, I will become broken over my sin of selfishness and self-absorption.

When my eyes are opened, my compassion for the misfortunate will be shaped into action rather than tears.

When my eyes are opened, my moments of depression will be replaced with hours of seeking you and pursuing a love relationship with you as much as you pursue me. I will no longer be an evasive lover. I will allow you to catch me and be intimate with me.

When my eyes are opened, I can hear your voice, for it is when my eyes are open, my ears are open.

When my eyes are opened, my daughter's concerns that once seemed trivial become as important to me as they are to her.

When my eyes are opened, my son's sensitivities are not pushed aside as a phase that will pass, but are looked upon as an opportunity to place another strong building block in his foundation.

When my eyes are opened, I will realize you are in control. I will seek your will and live at the center of your will. I will no longer try to lead myself. When I lead, I fall and stumble. I want you to lead rather than having to always rescue me from the mud of the path I have chosen. Father, please open my eyes.

Before my eyes were opened....

My life was filled with sorrow, and my "self" was in control.

My passion was not for God, it was for what this world had to offer.

My children played at my feet and grew up while I mindlessly ignored the beauty and missed the miracle.

I accumulated things but never satisfied the insatiable desire to own.

I obeyed God but never walked with Him.

I knew He had a son but I never knew Him.

My job was me, and my identity was my job.

I had a spouse, but did not treat her like a bride.

God blessed my wife with supernatural intuition that would have saved me much anguish, disappointment, money and hard lessons learned. I dismissed it as ignorant, over-concerns.

I trained others with advice for efficient living, but failed to see that efficiency without love, passion and a spirit led life is simply good time management, used to manage the wrong things.

Then, God opened my eyes.

When my eyes open...

My love relationship with God is not compartmentalized into "quiet time". It is the "only thing". It is what I "seek first", not an "additional interest" on my resume. It is what controls and guides my life.

My pains are turned to passions.

Evil is easily recognizable and cannot be disguised.

What this world has to offer is seen for what it is, "empty mindless pursuits", "chasing after the wind", and "influenced by Satan".

Watching TV is out; games with my children are in.

My spouse's intuition is prophetic words that guard me against my poor judgment.

Christ is the window to who God is. To know Him is to know God.

My role is not just the "bread winner", but...a child of God, father, husband, son, brother.

My love for God became passionate. Frequent moments of passion and a Spirit-filled life replaced my compartmentalized God.

Moments of depression are now seen as attacks by Satan. Prayer is prescribed over Prozac.

Humorous moments laughing with my wife and children sitting around the supper table replace hours sitting around the boardroom table with pretentious socialites seeking to manipulate time into profits.

Listening to God's voice and allowing Him to guide me has replaced self-motivational tapes and books, subliminal music, therapeutic mind manipulation, 10 Easy Steps to Wealth Accumulation, 10 Easy Steps to Raising Obedient Children, 10 Easy Steps to Unconditional Love, 10 Easy Steps to Overcoming a Dysfunctional Childhood, and 10 Easy Steps from Co-Dependence to Independence.

When my eyes are open...

My young daughter begins to teach me more about adult women. She teaches me how to understand my wife better.

My young son reminds me that I was once a sensitive male with feelings that could be hurt, that men do need to be hugged and kissed and loved. He reminds me as time rushes by, baby teeth are replaced with molars, pimples appear and shaving begins. I begin to chase him, rather than him chasing me. I soon learn I will only be able to catch him the same number of times I let him catch me.

When my eyes are open...

I will play more ball with my kids, and network less.

I will put down the TV remote and sit with folded legs on the floor with a game board between me and my young daughter.

I will show my children how to use the Internet, for efficiencies rather than mindless entertainment.

Fruits of the Spirit will appear in my life because I am filled with the Spirit, not because I have practiced or perfected keeping God's commands.

My God and Savior will say, "Come be with me, you have finished the race, I know you. Come on in and let me show you what we have built for you." I will feel the arms of my God and Savior around my neck. I will thank them for wanting to love me in spite of my sin. We will then dance together and celebrate victory.

When my eyes are opened, I will turn to you, you will lift the veil, I will see you face to face!

I can see you now. You are a living, personal dad.

There is nothing between us; my face is shining with the brightness of your glory.

Come into my life. Make me brighter and more beautiful. Make me like you! Make me free! (2 Cor. 3:17,18)

Keeping my eyes open is a journey, not a destination.

"I will give you a new heart and put a new spirit in you; I will remove from you your heart of stone and give you a heart of flesh. And I will put my Spirit in you and move you to follow my decrees and be careful to keep my laws."

(Ezek. 36: 26-27)

Moved by God

~⌒~

WHEN MEN LIKE you decide to find God, when faith barely burns above the wick, He answers with hope. He honors the smallest amount of belief, and gives men who receive Him a new spirit. He removes stubbornness and pride and hearts of stone. He moves men to a better place with a much wider perspective and with direction and understanding for a better life.

The journey to authenticity as men isn't easy for many of us. It requires faith while looking at giant problems, difficult times and our sinful condition. It requires us to leave everything behind as we depend upon the God who made us. It means that we persevere through and strive within the circumstances and challenges of life as we look to Him for power and direction.

When men are moved, it's as if stones are brought back to life from heaps of rubble. Men treat women differently and they rebuild the intimacy they lost years ago. They are courageous and no longer self-centered. They approach work with spiritual guidance and strength, and they give their very best for the benefit of others and the glory of God.

The hearts of godly men are moved by the presence of His Spirit within them. People see these men as strong and purposeful—givers, protectors, and not takers or slackers. God brings men out of waste and rubble and teaches them, through Jesus, to model and maintain His loving standards. He teaches men to rebuild the brokenness and ruins within a fallen world. God moves men as spiritual leaders into a meaningful life of service lived with faith in Jesus.

As authentic men put childish ways behind them, their talk changes and their love increases for the God who made them. No longer do they make as many desperate decisions. As they look back at their life story, they can see the signposts they followed that were written by the hand of God.

They talk with God. They listen for God. They even struggle with Him in the authenticity of their faith. Godly men can be trusted by God and by other men. They are childlike in their faith and committed to their responsibilities and to their families.

CHANGED BY HIM

Real men of God stop the behavioral cycle of past generations within their family. They rescue others from the grip of sin through the power of God evidenced in their own changed lives. Their authentic faith changes their actions and habits, as they bring God into the hidden part of their lives. They struggle with Him. They approach Him with honesty and openness, and because of this, these men win the trust of others and the favor of God and their lives are changed. This impact reverberates through family trees, friends and even business associates.

In all the ways of their lives, men of God acknowledge Him on the paths they choose to walk. They persevere. They lead. They follow Jesus wholeheartedly because they know the truth of his life, death and resurrection. They know God loves them because of the sacrifice of the greatest man who ever lived. They know who they are, what they stand for, and where to find strength, power and wisdom for the challenges they face. They pray and do it all with Him.

When it's time to step up and take on the Goliaths of this world, real men are present. They show courage and avoid the traps of this world. They gather together as men who need each other. In this fellowship they remember who they are and who they depend upon. They make the great decisions of life with much counsel and prayer. They increase in the wisdom of God throughout their lives.

Mighty men chase the things in this world that last and they make a difference for the glory of God and for the salvation of those around them. They rebuild the intimacy that was lost between themselves and God and men and women. They soar like eagles looking for the battles that matter to those in their care. They invest in what will make a positive difference and not in things of fleeting significance.

Men begin their days in the still quiet of the morning knowing that He is God. As a result, they hear His voice in the day and avoid the sirens that lure them into danger. They forgive those around them because when they remember Jesus, they realize He has forgiven them. They love children and shelter them from harm because they see the real authentic nature of their souls just forming. Men of God respond to a loving Father who made them in the beginning and now wants to walk with them from early morning till dark. Men begin their days with Him and do not forget who they are as time passes.

Because of Jesus and despite their own failures, sins and other inadequacies, men live in freedom, knowing that their God does not condemn them but instead saves them and changes them through the sacrifice of His Son. This brings confession and a humility that transforms them as they allow God to chip away at their old ways. The power of His unfathomable love brings godly change into their hearts and into their lives. So men do not mind admitting that idols are or have been a part of their lives, and they know Jesus is the only way that their lives have been redeemed and changed.

Men of God know that nothing can separate them from the love displayed by Jesus on a cross in Israel 2000 years ago. The story of Christ and the stories of godly men wind themselves together into garments that display the design of His intended masterpieces. The very Spirit of God changes men and reveals a piece of heaven and the victory assured for eternity by Jesus Christ.

I pray that you and the other men who read this book find a new life and a godly definition of manhood. I pray that your eyes are opened to see Him and He helps you know that you have "what it takes"—Jesus.